KOREAN STORIES

FOR LANGUAGE LEARNERS

JULIE DAMRON, Ph.D.
&
EUNSUN YOU, MA

TUTTLE Publishing

Tokyo | Rutland, Vermont | Singapore

Contents

Preface

As a university professor of Korean for many years, I have used numerous books with many different types of students. I have found lots of good Korean grammar books and online programs to use in my courses. Unfortunately, I struggled to find a reading book for true beginners. I wanted to use Korean stories in my classes so that we could discuss the culture that went along with the stories, but every Korean storybook reader that I found was for intermediate level or above. Although the authors claimed it was for beginners, none of them were appropriate for true beginner students. The passages were long, the sentence structures were advanced and the vocabulary was large and complicated. My beginning students asked for level-appropriate material to read in Korean because they felt passionate about reading beyond the functional text presented in their grammar books. It was for them that I started writing this beginning Korean reader.

Korean Stories for Language Learners can be used either by an individual who wants to learn to read and write in Korean or by an instructor in the Korean classroom. Chapters are self-contained and easy to follow. Instructions are in both English and Korean.

The early stories in this book are highly modified from their original version. They become increasingly less modified in later chapters. All chapters have vocabulary words written in Korean, Romanized Korean and in English. Each chapter contains the story written in Korean and pre- and post-reading activities. The book also contains extensive Korean and English glossaries.

At the end of this book a basic explanation of the sounds of Korean (vowels and consonants) is given. This instructs the reader on how to read and write those vowels, consonants and then syllables. The book provides plenty of writing practice for Korean letters before moving on to writing words. There is a helpful pronunciation activity that helps students distinguish between aspirated, tense and lax sounds. Finally, students learn to practice writing basic sentences.

I would like to acknowledge You Eunsun, my graduate student assistant and co-author. EunSun worked tirelessly to help find and modify the Korean folktales used in this book, all while taking courses in her master's program, teaching Korean and studying for her preliminary examination. She was an amazing asset to this work. I also want to thank my upper-level undergraduate students who edited various versions of this book, and my Korean 101 and 102 students who love studying Korean and whose avid passion for the language and culture prompted me to begin writing this book.

Thanks to Nancy Goh at Tuttle Publishing, to Megan Young who did the majority of the illustrations and to Kim Kyuri for the audio recordings.

Finally, I want to thank my supportive husband, Danny, and my loving kids, Leah, Andrew and Maya, who are the joy of my life.

—Julie Damron

A Brief Introduction to the Korean Language

안녕하세요! Annyeonghaseyo!

Welcome to *Korean Stories for Language Learners*! This book is designed to help you, a new learner of Korean, establish a foundation in the Korean language and develop a basic cultural understanding that you can then build on for years to come. No matter why you've decided to start learning Korean, you are in the right place! After learning to read and write in the first few chapters, you will begin building vocabulary by reading Korean folktales and applying this new knowledge as you begin speaking and writing. As you read, you will not only begin using the language, you will also begin to understand the history of Korean culture. In most countries—especially in a country as old as Korea—the language is closely tied to the culture and vice versa. Learning to appreciate the uniqueness of Korea will help you cultivate a passion for the language as you continue learning. It is often said that a foreigner will never learn to speak Korean well until they learn to love kimchi! You will find that as you build this passion for the people, culture, and history, you will discover a greater motivation to study. Look for ways to use the language as often as you can!

Understanding Korea

Before we dive into the fundamentals of the language, let's take a look at Korea as a whole. Korea is a beautiful country with a history seemingly as old as time. Today, the country is divided into the North and South: the Democratic People's Republic of Korea in the north and the Republic of Korea to the south. Although the governments of these two countries are often at odds, the majority of native Koreans dream of the day when their country will be unified once again. Since the end of the Korean War in 1953, both countries have experienced remarkable net growth, although since the 1970s South Korea has dramatically outpaced growth in the North.

Economic prosperity in South Korea has resulted in large population growth and the development of huge urban centers like Seoul and Busan. In 1942, toward the end of Japanese rule, the population of Korea was around 25 million. Today, 51 million Koreans live in South Korea and about 25 million live in the

North. If one includes Koreans living internationally, nearly 80 million people are native speakers of Korean. This makes it one of the most commonly spoken languages in the world.

Beginning in the 1990s, a growing awareness of and interest in the South Korean culture has led to an increase in collective international interest in learning Korean. This expanding sphere of influence held by Korean culture has been termed the "Korean Wave" (or 한류 **hanryu**), due in part to its sudden expansion. While the main catalyst for the spread of South Korean culture was originally the novelty of and interest in K-dramas and K-pop, Korea's history and traditional culture are beginning to receive international recognition as South Korea continues developing into a travel destination for local Asian tourists and others alike. Seoul, the largest city on the Korean peninsula and capital of South Korea, is home to around 25 million people. In other words, one out of every three Koreans lives in Seoul! Because the area around Seoul was settled over 6,000 years ago, serving as the capital for various kingdoms and empires throughout its history, the city of Seoul has developed into a thriving metropolis that blends traditional Korean culture with the advances of modernity. This unique atmosphere attracts millions of tourists every year, allowing foreigners to come and experience the Korean way. These millions of tourists have added a new component to the idea of the Korean Wave, as chefs and internationally minded visitors have returned to their countries with a craving for Korean cooking. The idea of fusion food, or the combining of two foods from different countries, is nothing new, and South Korea's rise has given way to dishes like the bulgogi burger and the kimchi burrito as restaurants have begun experimenting with the strong flavors unique to Korea. Understanding the Korean culture is crucial to developing a strong ability with the language, and there is no way to become more accustomed to the Korean culture than by learning to love the food.

The traditional Korean diet revolves around rice, vegetables, kimchi, **banchan** (assorted side dishes), and a hot pepper paste called **gochujang** (고추장). Even though fast food and other western foods have nearly taken over the diet of younger Koreans, traditional components remain central to the modern Korean diet. One reason the Korean culture is so closely tied to food is because of the traditions associated both with food preparation, and the seasons food is eaten. In November of each year, the country begins an enormous project called **Kimjang** (김장). *Kimjang* is the traditional process of preparing kimchi for the coming winter months. For weeks during this period, Koreans spend an enormous amount of time making kimchi and layering it in jars and refrigerators for preservation. Although the mass production of kimchi has led to fewer people participating in this process, for millions it is still an annual event to make kimchi, and some people even travel home to assist their parents in the labor-intensive process. The presence of Korean cuisine in the national culture is well established, and as with language learning in any country, learning to fully appreciate the culture makes a world of a difference when it comes to learning that country's language.

The Language

Located on the Korean Peninsula in northeast Asia, until about 70 years ago there was no concept of the country of "Korea" being divided into north and south. Before being occupied by the Japanese in the early 1900s, the entire peninsula was ruled as one country by different Korean dynasties. The first of these, the Koryo dynasty, was founded in 918 and continued to 1392, corresponding to the High Middle Ages in Europe and the First Crusade to Jerusalem. "Koryo" (also written as "Goryeo") is actually where the westernized word "Korea" comes from. After the Koryo dynasty fell in 1392, the Joseon dynasty came into power. The Kingdom of Joseon is considered one of history's greatest dynasties because it lasted for 505 years, making it one of the longest uninterrupted states in world history. This long period of stability allowed for the pursuit of scientific invention, developing iconic works of literature and art like the Sijo, and even the invention of the Korean writing system, **Hangeul** (한글).

Before Hangeul's invention, the Korean language was written using Chinese characters. These characters were modified for communicating in Korean using systems like **hyangchal** (향찰), **gugyeol** (구결), and **idu** (이두). Since one had to learn the thousands of characters to be literate, writing and obtaining an education were reserved for the wealthy and high class, known as **Yangban** (양반).

Chinese characters are known in Korea as **Hanja** (한자) and are important for several reasons. The use of Chinese characters as a writing system, along with Korea's close proximity to China, exposed educated Koreans to the Chinese language. As a result, anywhere from 30% to 65% (estimates vary) of Korean vocabulary is based on Chinese roots. Such words are called Sino-Korean, and share the meaning of the Chinese characters from which they originated. The vast majority of the remaining vocabulary is native Korean, with an increasing number of loan words being borrowed from English, German, and Japanese. Increasing globalization has lead to the introduction of new ideas into Korea, and often to the introduction into the Korean language of foreign words used to describe these ideas. One example of this is the German word for "work", *arbeit*, which is written in Korean as 아르바이트 [areubaiteu] and means "part-time work." Understanding the roots of the words you learn will be critical for understanding and using the Korean language. As you grow your Sino-Korean vocabulary, you will find that you recognize the meanings of new words that share the same roots. As you develop your native Korean vocabulary, you will find that you have a stronger understanding of the grammar and traditions of Korea.

Hangeul

Originally named **Hunminjeongeum** (훈민정음), Hangeul, also transcribed as "Hangul," is called **Joseon** writing in North Korea (조선글 **joseongeul**). It is a writing system unlike any other. While most other systems of writing (like the English alphabet, the Chinese logograms, and the Japanese syllabary) evolved over hundreds and even thousands of years, the modern Korean alphabet of Hangeul was invented by a group of scholars commissioned by King Sejong of the Joseon dynasty in 1444. Now considered one of Korea's greatest rulers, King Sejong understood the value of literacy, and formulated a plan to give his people the ability to read and write. Although Hangeul is now the official script of both North and South Korea, it was some time before it was recognized as legitimate by all Koreans, and even longer for it to be implemented in official documents. After the script was introduced, the system experienced pushback from educated elites who still believed Hanja to be the only true writing system. Hangeul was even briefly banned in 1504 by a king who didn't want to see information quickly distributed. However, it was revived in the late 16th century, as Korean poetry such as **gasa** (가사) and **sijo** (시조) began being written in Hangeul. Popular support for Hangeul continued to grow as Korean novels grew in popularity, and was solidified when it became tied to the Korean nationalism movement in the 19th and 20th centuries. The 1890s saw a particularly strong push for widened usage, as the first official document using Hangeul was created in 1884, and with elementary school texts incorporating the script in 1895. The next year, in 1896, the *Dongnip Sinmun* (독립신문), the first newspaper in Hangeul, began to be published.

During the Japanese occupation, Japanese became the official language of the Korean peninsula. However, native Koreans continued writing with the script, preserving it throughout the colonial period. After the war, Hangeul was standardized and updated for modern life. Although the separation of the North and South Koreans has led to the development of certain differences in vocabulary, pronunciation, and spelling, the characters used by Koreans in the North and the South remain the same.

Now that we know where Hangeul came from, let's take a closer look at the alphabet. Hangeul is composed of 40 characters (letters) that are combined in all sorts of different ways to form words. In modern Hangeul, there are 19 consonants and 21 vowels. These symbols make up what is called a phonetic alphabet, just like the English alphabet. For example, in order to write "bag" in English, the letters "b-a-g" are put together. Similarly, in order to write "bag," pronounced "kabang" in Korean, the letters "ㄱ – ㅏ – ㅂ – ㅏ – ㅇ" are put together. Ten of the vowels in Korean are simple vowels or "basic" vowels such as the English "a" sound. All of the rest of the vowels come from combining two basic vowels such as the "ai" sound in the English word "pie." This may seem pretty complex now, but as you practice and memorize the Korean letters, you will find it useful to understand how they are formed.

There are fewer consonants and they are less complex. There are 10 basic consonants and when we put two consonants together we end up with 19 total consonants. In an effort to help the commoners of his time learn these consonants, King Sejong actually designed the consonants to imitate the shape your tongue and mouth make when you say them. For example the English sound "k" in Korean looks like "ㄱ" and is supposed to represent what your tongue looks like when you make the sound. Try it. When you make the "k" sound, does your tongue look like the Korean symbol "ㄱ"? We will discuss the vowels and consonants in detail on page 184 but you will find that they are easy to learn. Diligence is going to serve you well as you begin learning Korean. And, while there is much more to say about Korea and how the language came to be, it's time to dive in. Memorize, recite, read, speak, listen, write, practice, and keep with it!

You're going to do great.

Once again, welcome to *Korean Stories for Language Learners*!

Reference

"The Best Alphabet in the World," Robin Hansen.

새로운 친구들 만나기

Saeloun Chingudeul Mannagi

소피아: 안녕하세요. 제 이름은 소피아입니다. 저는 미국 사람입니다.
민수:　반갑습니다. 제 이름은 민수입니다. 저는 한국 사람입니다.
소피아: 민수 씨, 안녕히 가세요.
민수:　안녕히 가세요.

❖ ❖ ❖

Meeting New Friends

❖ *Learn to use simple greetings.* ❖

Sophia:　Hello. My name is Sophia. I am American.
Minsu:　Nice to meet you. My name is Minsu. I am Korean.

———

Sophia:　Mr. Minsu, goodbye.
Minsu:　Goodbye!

❖ ❖ ❖

Vocabulary

안녕하세요 **annyeonghaseyo** hello
제 **je** my
이름 **ileum** name
저 **jeo** I
미국 **migug** America
사람 **salam** a person

반갑습니다 **bangabseubnida**
　nice to meet you
한국 **hangug** Korea
씨 **ssi** Mr. (or Mrs.)
안녕히 가세요 **annyeonghi**
　gaseyo goodbye

Comprehension Questions

a. Where is 소피아 from?
b. Where is 민수 from?
c. How do you say "hello" in Korean?
d. How do you say "goodbye" in Korean?

Writing Activity

You just met a Korean friend. You need to say "hi" and introduce yourself.
Write "hello," your name, and where you are from.

내 친구, 민수

Nae Chingu, Minsu

민수는 학생입니다. 민수는 아침에 일찍 일어납니다. 민수는 아침밥을 먹고 학교에 갑니다. 민수는 소피아를 만났습니다. "안녕하세요?" 소피아가 인사합니다. "안녕하세요." 민수도 인사합니다. 민수와 소피아는 학교에 가서 공부를 합니다.

❖ ❖ ❖

My Friend, Minsu

❖ *This story is about a student, Minsu.* ❖

Minsu is a student. Minsu wakes up early. Minsu eats breakfast and goes to school. Minsu met Sophia. "Hello," Sophia says hi. "Hello," Minsu says hi, too. Minsu and Sophia go to school and study.

❖ ❖ ❖

Vocabulary

학생 **hagsaeng** a student

아침 **achim** morning

일찍 **iljjig** early

아침밥 **achimbab** breakfast

학교 **haggyo** a school

먹다 **meogda** to eat

가다 **gada** to go

만나다 **mannada** to meet

인사하다 **insahada** to greet

공부 **gongbu** to study

Comprehension Questions

a. Is 민수 a student?

b. What did 민수 do before going to school?

c. Who did 민수 meet on the way to school?

d. What did 민수 and 소피아 do at school?

Writing Activity

Write about what you usually do in the morning.

동물의 왕 여우

Dongmul-ui Wang Yeou

어느 날 여우가 숲 속을 걷고 있었습니다. 갑자기 호랑이가 나타났습니다. 여우는 호랑이가 무서웠습니다. 하지만 여우는 호랑이에게 말했습니다.

"내가 무섭지? 나는 동물의 왕이야!"

호랑이는 믿지 않았습니다. 여우는 호랑이에게 자기 뒤를 따라오라고 말했습니다.

동물들이 여우 뒤의 호랑이를 보고 달아났습니다. 호랑이는 여우가 동물의 왕이라고 믿었습니다.

❖ ❖ ❖

The Fox Who is the King of Animals

❖ *This story is about a clever fox.* ❖

One day, a fox was walking in the forest. Suddenly, a tiger appeared. The fox was afraid of the tiger. However, the fox said to the tiger, "Aren't you afraid of me? I am the king of animals!" The tiger did not believe the fox. The fox told the tiger to follow behind him.

The animals ran away as soon as they saw the tiger behind the fox. The tiger believed that the fox was truly the king.

❖ ❖ ❖

Pre-Reading Questions (answer in Korean or English)

a. 제목을 보세요. 여우가 동물의 왕입니까?

Look at the title. Do you agree with the idea that the fox is the king of all the animals?

b. 여우는 옛날 이야기에서 보통 어떤 성격을 가지고 있습니까?

What are common characteristics that foxes have in folktales?

Vocabulary

동물 **dongmul** animal

왕 **wang** a king

여우 **yeou** a fox

어느 날 **eoneunal** one day

숲 속 **sup sog** in the forest

걷다 **geod-da** to walk

갑자기 **gabjagi** suddenly

호랑이 **horang-i** a tiger

나타나다 **natanada** to appear

무섭다 **museobda** scared

하지만 **hajiman** however

말하다 **malhada** to say

믿지 않다 **midji anta** to not believe

뒤 **dwi** behind

따라오다 **daraoda** to follow

보다 **boda** to see

달아나다 **dalanada** to run away

믿다 **mid-da** to believe

Culture Notes

In Korean traditional folktales, the fox usually appeared as an animal that was smart and very good at deception. In some stories, foxes get out of dangerous situations by deceiving others. In other stories, they deceive others to prey on them or to put them in danger. In Korean society, like most societies, people who behave like a "fox" should always be avoided.

Comprehension Questions

a. 이 이야기 속 여우는 정말 동물의 왕입니까?

Is the fox in this story really the king of all the animals?

b. 동물들은 왜 여우를 보고 도망갔습니까?

Why did the animals see and then run away from the fox?

c. 여우는 왜 거짓말을 했습니까?

Why did the fox lie?

Writing Activity

If you were the fox in the story, how would you escape from the tiger?

밤에게 절을 한 호랑이

Bam-ege Jeol-eul Han Holang-i

어느 날 호랑이가 산 속을 걷고 있었습니다. 호랑이는 아주 배가 고팠습니다. 그때 호랑이는 고슴도치를 보았습니다. 호랑이는 고슴도치를 깨물었습니다. 고슴도치의 가시 때문에 호랑이는 아팠습니다. 호랑이는 고슴도치를 먹을 수 없었습니다. 호랑이는 계속 배가 고팠습니다. 호랑이는 산 속을 걷다가 밤송이를 보았습니다. 호랑이는 밤송이를 보고 고슴도치라고 생각했습니다. 호랑이는 무서웠습니다. 그래서 밤송이에게 절을 했습니다.

❖ ❖ ❖

The Tiger Who Bowed to the Chestnut

❖ *This story is about a poor tiger who was scared of a hedgehog.* ❖

One day, a tiger was walking in the forest. The tiger was very hungry. Just then, the tiger saw a hedgehog. The tiger bit the hedgehog. The tiger was hurt because of the hedgehog's quills. The tiger could not eat the hedgehog. The tiger was still hungry. The tiger saw a chestnut burr while walking in the forest. The tiger thought that the chestnut burr was a hedgehog. The tiger was scared, so he bowed to the chestnut.

❖ ❖ ❖

Pre-Reading Questions (answer in Korean or English)

a. 호랑이가 밤을 무서워합니까? Are tigers afraid of chestnuts?
b. 밤송이를 본 적이 있습니까? 어떻게 생겼습니까?
   Have you ever seen a chestnut burr (outer shell of a chestnut)? What does
   it look like?

Vocabulary

어느 날 **eoneu nal** one day
호랑이 **horang-i** a tiger
산 속 **san sog** in the forest
걷다 **geod-da** to walk
배가 고프다 **baega gopeuda** hungry
그때 **geu ddae** at that time
고슴도치 **goseumdochi** hedgehog
보다 **boda** to see
산 속 **san soge** in the mountains
깨물다 **ggaemulda** to bite
가시 **gasi** quill

아주 **aju** very, so
아프다 **apeuda** to hurt
먹을 수 없다 **meugeul su eobda**
   cannot eat
계속 **gyesok** still
밤송이 **bamsong-i** chestnut burr
~라고 생각하다 **lago sang-**
   gakada to think something
무섭다 **museobda** scared
그래서 **geuraeseo** so
절을 하다 **jeol-eul hada** to bow

Culture Notes

In real life, tigers are very dangerous animals. However, in Korean traditional folktales
tigers are depicted as foolish and slow. This is because tigers used to be commonly seen
in Korea and were not necessarily feared. However, they were still dangerous animals
that men could not beat. This dichotomy led writers to portray tigers as being funny and
humorous in stories.

Comprehension Questions

a. 호랑이는 왜 고슴도치를 먹지 못했습니까?
   Why couldn't the tiger eat the hedgehog?
b. 호랑이는 밤송이를 보고 무엇이라고 생각했습니까?
   What did the tiger think when he saw the chestnut burr?
c. 호랑이는 왜 밤송이에게 절을 했습니까?
   Why did the tiger bow to the chestnut burr?

Writing Activity

Have you ever misjudged someone or something because of an outer appearance? Write
about a similar experience that you have had.

잠꾸러기 아기 곰

Jamkkuleogi Agi Gom

한 아기 곰이 숲속에 살았습니다. 그가 늦잠을 잤고 학교에 늦게 갔습니다. 그의 반 친구들은 그를 놀렸습니다. 그가 그의 얼굴을 씻지 않았기 때문이었습니다. 그가 연못으로 갔고 그의 얼굴을 씻었습니다. 그의 얼굴이 깨끗해졌습니다. 그가 연못을 보고 웃었습니다. 연못도 그에게 웃어주었습니다.

❖ ❖ ❖

A Sleepyhead Baby Bear

❖ *This story is about a baby bear that was a sleepyhead.* ❖

A baby bear lived in the forest. He slept in and went to school late. His classmates teased him. They teased him because he didn't wash his face. He went to a pond and washed his face. His face became clean. He smiled at the pond. The pond smiled back at him.

❖ ❖ ❖

Pre-Reading Questions (answer in Korean or English)

a. 제목을 보세요. 이 이야기가 무엇에 관한 이야기라고 생각합니까?
   Look at the title. What do you think this story is about?
b. 당신의 나라에는 아기곰 이야기가 있습니까?
   Does your country have a story about baby bears?

Vocabulary

아기 곰 **agigome** a baby bear
숲 속에 **sup soge** in the forest
늦게 잤다 **neukke jatta** to sleep late
   (past tense)
학교 **hakgyo** a school
늦게 갔다 **neukke gatta** to go late
   (past tense)
반 친구들 **ban chingudeul** classmates

놀리다 **nolida** to tease
씻지 않다 **ssitjianta** to not wash
얼굴 **eolgul** face
갔다 **gatta** to go (past tense)
연못 **yeonmot** pond
깨끗해지다 **kkae kkeut haejida**
   to become clean
웃다 **utta** to smile

Comprehension Questions

a. 곰이 어디에서 살았습니까? Where did the bear live?
b. 곰이 왜 늦었습니까? Why was the bear late?
c. 누가 곰을 놀렸습니까? Who teased the bear?
d. 곰이 무엇을 했습니까? What did the bear do?

Writing Activity

Many years have passed since this story. Now the bear is grown up. Write about where you think the bear is and what he is doing now. What has he accomplished?

당나귀와 메뚜기

Dangnagwiwa Mettugi

메뚜기가 나무 위에서 노래를 부르고 있었습니다. 당나귀는 메뚜기처럼 노래를 잘 하고 싶었습니다. 당나귀가 메뚜기에게 물어봤습니다. "노래를 잘 하기 위해서 무엇을 먹니? 메뚜기가 대답했습니다. "나는 이슬만 먹어." 당나귀는 이슬만 먹기 시작했습니다. 며칠 뒤, 그가 아팠고 죽었습니다.

❖ ❖ ❖

The Donkey and the Grasshopper

❖ *This story is about a donkey who wants to sing well—
like a grasshopper.* ❖

A grasshopper was singing in a tree. A donkey wanted to sing well like the grasshopper. The donkey asked the grasshopper, "What do you eat to sing so well?" The grasshopper answered, "I only eat dew." The donkey started only eating dew. A few days later, he got sick and died.

❖ ❖ ❖

Pre-Reading Questions (answer in Korean or English)

a. 이야기를 훑어보세요. 무엇에 관한 이야기라고 생각합니까?
   Scan through the story. What do you think this story is about?

b. 이야기의 배경이 무엇이라고 생각합니까?
   What do you think the setting of the story is?

c. 이야기의 교훈이 무엇일 것이라고 생각합니까?
   What do you think the moral of the story is?

Vocabulary

메뚜기 **mettugi** a grasshopper

노래를 부르다 **noraereul buruda**
   to sing

나무 **namu** tree

당나귀 **dangnagui** a donkey

노래를 잘 하다 **noraereul jal hada**
   to sing well

원하다 **wonhada** to want

물어보다 **mureoboda** to ask

먹다 **meokda** to eat

이슬 **i-seul** dew

며칠 뒤 **myeochil dui** a few days later

아프다 **apeuda** to get sick

죽다 **jukda** to die

Comprehension Questions

a. 메뚜기가 무엇을 잘 하였습니까? What did the grasshopper do well?

b. 당나귀가 무엇을 잘하고 싶어 했습니까? What did the donkey want to do well?

c. 당나귀가 무엇을 물어봤습니까? What did the donkey ask about?

d. 메뚜기가 먹는 것은 무엇입니까? What did the grasshopper eat?

e. 당나귀에게 무슨 일이 일어났습니까? What happened to the donkey?

Writing Activity

Write a few sentences about the moral of the story. Then discuss it with your classmates.

호랑이와 토끼

Holang-iwa Tokki

한 배고픈 호랑이가 토끼를 봤습니다. 호랑이는 토끼를 먹고 싶었습니다. 토끼가 말했습니다, "내가 당신에게 따뜻한 떡을 줄게요. 떡을 먼저 드세요. 그 다음에 나를 나중에 드세요."

그래서 호랑이는 기다렸습니다. 토끼가 돌을 한 개 가져와서 그 돌을 구웠습니다. 호랑이는 그 돌이 떡이라고 생각했습니다. 그는 그 돌을 먹었습니다. 이것은 너무 뜨거웠습니다. 호랑이가 울었습니다. 그는 토끼를 먹을 수 없었습니다.

❖ ❖ ❖

The Tiger and the Rabbit

❖ *This story is about a smart rabbit.* ❖

A hungry tiger saw a rabbit. The tiger wanted to eat the rabbit. The rabbit said, "I'll give you a warm rice cake. Eat the rice cake first, then eat me later." So the tiger waited. The rabbit brought a stone and grilled the rice cake. The tiger thought the stone was a rice cake. He ate it. It was too hot. The tiger cried. He couldn't eat the rabbit.

❖ ❖ ❖

Pre-Reading Questions (answer in Korean or English)

a. 호랑이와 토끼 중에 누가 더 똑똑합니까?

   Which is smarter: a tiger or a rabbit?

b. 호랑이가 무엇을 원한다고 생각합니까?

   What do you think the tiger wants?

c. 이 이야기가 어떻게 끝날 것이라고 생각합니까?

   How do you think this story ends?

Vocabulary

배고프다 **baegopeuda** to be hungry

호랑이 **horang-i** a tiger

토끼 **tokki** a rabbit

원하다 **wonhada** to want

먹다 **meokda** to eat

주다 **juda** to give

따뜻한 떡 **ttatteut-han tteok** a warm rice cake

나중에 **najung-e** later

기다리다 **gidarida** to wait

가져오다 **gajeo-oda** to bring

돌 **dol** a stone

굽다 **gubda** a grill

뜨겁다 **tteugeobda** to be hot

울다 **ulda** to cry

Culture Notes

Do you know how to make rice cakes (**tteok**)? Rice cakes can be made by grinding rice into fine powder and then steaming the pancake-shaped patties. In Korea, it is believed that the Korean people have been eating rice cakes ever since the Agricultural Age. There is a Korean proverb that says, "rice cakes on rice." We use this proverb when someone has enough food to be satisfied yet they get even more! They don't have anything more to ask for or want. This proverb shows that Korean people think rice cakes are more delicious than rice.

Comprehension Questions

a. 호랑이가 무엇을 원했습니까? What did the tiger want?

b. 토끼가 그에게 뭐라고 말했습니까? What did the rabbit say to him?

c. 호랑이가 어떤 실수를 했습니까? What mistake did the tiger make?

d. 호랑이가 어떻게 느꼈습니까? How did the tiger feel?

Writing Activity

Write a short journal entry from the perspective of the tiger. How did his day go after this incident and how was he feeling later that evening?

아버지와 그의 두 딸들

Abeojiwa Geuui Du Ttaldeul

한 아버지와 두 딸이 있었습니다. 그는 그의 딸들을 아주 많이 사랑했습니다. 첫째 딸이 농부와 결혼했습니다. 둘째 딸은 도예가와 결혼했습니다. 어느 날, 아버지가 첫째 딸에게 무엇을 원하는지 물어봤습니다. 그가 신에게 그녀의 소원을 위해 기도하겠다고 말했습니다. 첫째 딸은 남편의 농장을 위해 비가 내리기를 원했습니다. 그가 둘째 딸에게 똑같은 질문을 했습니다. 그녀는 남편의 일을 위해 날씨가 항상 화창하기를 원했습니다. 아버지는 무엇을 위해 기도해야 할지 몰랐습니다.

❖ ❖ ❖

A Father and His Two Daughters

❖ *This story is about a father who loves his two daughters equally.* ❖

There was a father who had two daughters. He loved his daughters very much. The first daughter married a farmer. The second daughter married a potter. One day, the father asked the first daughter what she wanted. He said he would pray to God for her wish. The first daughter wished rain to fall for her husband's farm. He asked the same question to his second daughter. She wished the weather would always be sunny for her husband's work.

The father did not know which wish to pray for!

❖ ❖ ❖

Pre-Reading Questions (answer in Korean or English)

a. 이 이야기가 무엇에 관한 이야기라고 생각하십니까?

   What do you think the story is about?

b. 어떤 소원이 있습니까?

   What wishes do you have?

c. 어떤 날씨를 좋아합니까?

   What is your favorite kind of weather?

Vocabulary

농부 **nongbu** a farmer

도예가 **doyega** a potter

소원 **sowon** a wish

농장 **nongjang** a farm

비 **bi** rain

똑같은 **ttok-kat'un** same

질문 **jilmoon** a question

날씨 **nalssi** weather

화창하다 **hwachanghada** sunny

기도하다 **gidohada** to pray

원하다 **wonhada** to wish

Culture Notes

What wish should a father pray for if he had two daughters with conflicting interests? In Korean traditional folktales, there are many occasions where two interests conflict. Sometimes one side is good and the other side is not, and sometimes in Korean folktales one must die for the other to survive. In this story, we see only the father's dilemma. It shows that there are often occasions when differing interests—either good or bad—conflict.

Comprehension Questions

a. 아버지는 왜 딸들에게 소원을 물어봤습니까?

   Why did the father ask his daughters for their wishes?

b. 첫째 딸의 소원은 무엇이었습니까?

   What was the first daughter's wish?

c. 둘째 딸의 소원은 무엇이었습니까?

   What was the second daughter's wish?

d. 왜 아버지는 어떤 기도를 할지 몰랐습니까?

   Why didn't the father know what to pray for?

Writing Activity

Write a few sentences about the moral of the story. Then discuss it with your classmates.

방귀 시합

Bang-gwi Sihab

옛날에 방귀를 잘 뀌는 사람이 두 명 있었습니다. 한 명은 여자였고, 다른 한 명은 남자였습니다. 두 사람은 서로 다른 마을에 살았습니다. 남자가 여자의 집에 가서 방귀 시합을 하자고 했습니다. 여자는 항아리를 가져와 방귀를 뀌었습니다. 항아리가 남자 쪽으로 날아갔습니다. 남자도 항아리에 방귀를 뀌었습니다. 항아리가 여자 쪽으로 날아갔습니다. 여자도 다시 항아리에 방귀를 뀌었습니다. 두 사람은 하루 종일 방귀를 뀌었습니다. 하지만 아무도 이기지 못했습니다. 두 사람은 시합을 포기했습니다.

❖ ❖ ❖

The Farting Match

❖ *This story is about two people who fart really well.* ❖

Long ago, there were two people who farted very well. One was a woman, and the other was a man. They lived in two different villages from each other. One day, the man went to the woman's house and said, "Let's have a farting match." The woman brought a pot and farted in it. The pot flew toward the man. The man farted in the pot, too. The pot flew back to the woman. The woman farted in the pot again.

The man and woman farted all day long. However, nobody won. They gave up the match.

❖ ❖ ❖

Pre-Reading Questions (answer in Korean or English)

a. 다른 사람 앞에서 방귀를 뀌어 본 적이 있습니까?

   Have you ever farted in front of other people?

b. 시합하는 것을 좋아합니까? Do you enjoy competition?

c. 방귀시합에서 누가 이겼을까요? In a farting match, would you probably win?

Vocabulary

방귀 **bang-gwi** a fart

시합 **sihap** a match

두 명 **du myeong** two people

한 명 **han myeong** one person

여자 **yeoja** a woman

남자 **namja** a man

서로 **seoro** each other

다른 **dareun** different

마을 **ma-eul** a village

집 **jip** a house

살다 **sal-da** to live

하자고 하다 **hajago hada**

   to say let's do something

항아리 **hang-ari** a pot

방귀를 뀌다 **bang-gwileur kkwida**

   to fart

쪽 **jjok** side

날아가다 **nal-agada** to fly

하루 종일 **harujong-il** all day long

아무도 **amudo** nobody

이기다 **igida** to win

포기하다 **pogihada** to give up

Culture Notes

Have you seen a **hang-ari** (china pot)? A **hang-ari** is made from clay. It is a Korean traditional jar that is narrow at the top and the bottom, and wide in the middle. Korean people have stored kimchi, red pepper paste (**Gochujang**), soybean paste (**doenjang**), and other Korean traditional condiments in them since ancient times. Nowadays, **hang-ari** are not as commonly used as before. However, houses in the Korean countryside still have them.

Comprehension Questions

a. 두 사람은 왜 방귀 시합을 했습니까?

   Why did the two people in the story have the farting match?

b. 방귀 시합에서 먼저 방귀를 뀐 사람은 누구입니까?

   Who farted first in the farting match?

c. 누가 먼저 방귀 시합을 하자고 했습니까?

   Who said, "Let's have a farting match"?

d. 두 사람은 왜 시합을 포기했습니까?

   Why did the two people give up the match?

Writing Activity

Write a few sentences about your experiences related to farts.

해님 달님

Haenim Dalnim

옛날에 한 엄마가 있었습니다. 그녀는 돈이 없었습니다. 엄마는 아들과 딸과 함께 숲에서 살았습니다. 어느 날 한 호랑이가 나타났습니다. 호랑이는 엄마에게 떡을 달라고 했습니다. 엄마는 호랑이에게 떡을 하나 주었습니다. 하지만 호랑이는 더욱 더 많은 떡을 원했습니다. 곧 모든 떡이 없어졌습니다. 그래서 호랑이는 엄마를 먹었습니다. 그는 그 아이들도 먹고 싶었습니다. 그래서 호랑이는 엄마 옷을 입었습니다. 호랑이가 엄마의 집으로 갔습니다. 그러나 호랑이는 꼬리를 가리지 않았습니다. 아이들이 호랑이의 꼬리를 봤습니다. 아이들이 밖으로 도망갔습니다. 아이들이 나무 꼭대기로 올라갔습니다. 호랑이가 나무를 자르려고 시도했습니다. 아이들이 기도를 했습니다. 한 줄이 하늘에서부터 내려왔습니다. 아이들이 줄을 타고 하늘로 올라갔습니다. 호랑이도 그 줄을 원했습니다. 다른 줄이 하늘에서 내려왔습니다. 그러나 호랑이의 줄은 망가져서 호랑이가 바닥으로 떨어졌습니다. 오늘 날, 하늘로 올라간 딸은 해가 되고 아들은 달이 되었습니다.

❖ ❖ ❖

The Sun and the Moon

❖ *This story is about a greedy tiger,*
a generous mother, and her two children. ❖

A long time ago, there was a mother. She had no money. She lived with her son and daughter in the forest. One day a tiger appeared. He wanted her rice cakes. She gave him one rice cake. Later he wanted more and more rice cakes. Soon the rice cakes were all gone, so, the tiger ate the mother. He wanted to eat the children, so he wore the mother's clothes. He went to the house, but he didn't cover his tail. The children saw his tail. They ran outside. They went to the top of a tree. The tiger tried to cut the tree down. The children prayed. A rope came down from heaven. They climbed up the rope. The tiger wanted a rope. Another rope came down from heaven, but his rope broke. He fell to the ground. Now the children are safe. Today, the girl is the sun. The boy is the moon.

❖ ❖ ❖

Pre-Reading Questions (answer in Korean or English)

a. 단어를 보세요. 단어에 관해 질문이 있습니까?

Look at the list of words. Do you have any questions about the vocabulary?

b. 이 이야기가 무엇에 관한 이야기라고 생각합니까?

What do you think this story is about?

c. 여러분의 나라에 비슷한 이야기가 있습니까?

Does your country have a similar story?

Vocabulary

어머니 **eomeoni** a mother

돈 **don** money

아들 **adeul** a son

딸 **ttal** a daughter

호랑이 **horang-i** a tiger

숲 **sup** a forest

나타나다 **natanada** to appear

떡 **tteok** rice cake

옷 **ot** clothes

집 **jip** a house

꼬리 **kkori** tail

먹다 **meokda** to eat

입다 **ipda** to wear

밖 **bak** outside

나무 **namu** a tree

자르다 **jareuda** to cut down

기도하다 **gidohada** to pray

하늘 **haneul** heaven

줄 **jul** a rope

망가지다 **mang-gajida** to break

떨어지다 **tteoreojida** to fall

해 **hae** sun

문 **mun** moon

올라가다 **ollagada** to climb

Culture Notes

This folktale tells a story of the creation of the sun and the moon. It's also about sibling love. It takes place in a time when only the stars existed, before the dawning of the Sun and the Moon. It tells of a poor peasant woman, who sold rice cakes for a living. In the end, we learn an important Korean moral: When you want something badly enough, you'll find a way to receive it if your intentions are good, kind and pure.

Comprehension Questions

a. 호랑이가 무엇을 원했습니까? What did the tiger want?

b. 엄마가 무엇을 주었습니까? What did the mother give?

c. 호랑이가 무엇을 먹었습니까? What did the tiger eat?

d. 아이들은 무서워했습니다. 그들이 무엇을 했습니까?

The children were scared. What did they do?

e. 오늘 날 무엇이 그 딸입니까? 무엇이 그 아들입니까?

According to the folktale, what is the girl now? What is the boy?

Writing Activity

Rewrite the story from the tiger's point of view. What did the tiger want? Were the tiger's actions wrong? What happened after his rope broke? Where is he now?

효자 호랑이

Hyoja Holang-i

옛날에 나무꾼이 나무를 베고 있었습니다. 한 호랑이가 갑자기 나타났습니다. 나무꾼은 무서워했습니다. 나무꾼은 호랑이에게 거짓말을 했습니다. 나무꾼이 말했습니다, "당신은 저의 형제입니다. 당신은 몇 년 전에 죽었고, 호랑이로 다시 태어났습니다."

호랑이는 나무꾼이 한 말을 믿었습니다. 호랑이는 그를 보내주었습니다. 호랑이는 나무꾼의 집에 한 달에 두 번씩 멧돼지를 가져다주었습니다. 어느 날, 나무꾼의 어머니가 죽었습니다. 호랑이는 그녀가 자신의 어머니라고 믿었습니다. 호랑이는 너무 슬펐고 며칠동안 아무것도 먹지 않았습니다. 호랑이는 슬픔 속에서 죽었습니다.

❖ ❖ ❖

The Filial Tiger

❖ *This story is about an innocent tiger who believes a woodcutter's lie.* ❖

Long ago, a woodcutter was cutting wood. A tiger suddenly appeared. The woodcutter was scared. He lied to the tiger and said, "You are my brother. You died a few years ago and were born again as a tiger." The tiger believed what the woodcutter said. The tiger let him go. The tiger brought a boar twice a month to the woodcutter's house. One day, the woodcutter's mother died. The tiger believed that she was his mother. The tiger was so sad and did not eat anything for a few days. The tiger died of grief.

❖ ❖ ❖

Pre-Reading Questions (answer in Korean or English)

a. 어떤 동물이 무섭습니까? What kind of animals are scary to you?

b. 효자가 무엇이라고 생각하십니까? What do you think filial piety is?

c. 언제 가장 큰 슬픔을느꼈습니까? When did you feel the greatest sorrow?

Vocabulary

나무꾼 **namukkun** a woodcutter

무서워하다 **museoweohada** to be scared

거짓말 **geojinmal** a lie

태어나다 **tae-eo-nada** to be born

멧돼지 **metdwaeji** a boar

믿다 **mitda** to believe

효자 **hyoja** filial

슬픔 **seulpeum** grief

옛날에 **yetnal-e** once upon a time

베다 **beda** to cut down

호랑이 **horang-i** a tiger

말하다 **malhada** to say

형제 **hyeong-je** a sibling

죽다 **jukda** to die

보내주다 **bonaejuda** to let someone go

한 달 **han dal** one month

가져다주다 **gajyeodajuda** to bring

며칠 **myeo-chil** a couple of days

Culture Notes

In Korea, filial piety (**hyo-do**) or respect for your parents or elders has been considered very important from ancient times. In this story, we meet a tiger who is loyal to a woodcutter's mother because the tiger believes she is his mother. There is a saying in Korea: "Grass grows on rocks if filial piety is utmost." In other words, if there is genuine filial piety (genuine respect), God will be touched and make the impossible come true.

Comprehension Questions

a. 나무꾼이 호랑이에게 왜 거짓말을 했습니까?
Why did the woodcutter lie to the tiger?

b. 나무꾼이 호랑이에게 어떤 거짓말을 했습니까?
What was the lie that the woodcutter told the tiger?

c. 호랑이가 왜 죽었습니까?
Why did the tiger die?

d. 호랑이에게서 어떤 것을 배울 수 있습니까?
What did you learn from the tiger?

Writing Activity

Write a few sentences about the moral of the story. Then discuss it with your classmates.

호랑이와 곶감

Holang-iwa Gokkam

산 속에 작은 마을이 있었습니다. 그 산에는 호랑이가 있었습니다. 어느 겨울 저녁, 그 호랑이는 배가 고팠습니다. 그는 음식을 찾기 위해 그 마을로 들어갔습니다. 그가 한 집에 갔고 밖에서 멈춰섰습니다. 그 집 안에서 한 아이가 울고 있었습니다. 엄마는 그 울음을 멈추게 하려고 시도했습니다. 엄마가 말했습니다, "봐! 여우야! 그가 와서 너를 먹을거야!" 아이는 울음을 멈추지 않았습니다.

엄마가 다시 시도했습니다. "봐! 곰이야! 그가 와서 너를 먹을거야!" 아이는 울음을 멈추지 않았습니다.

엄마가 말했습니다, "봐! 호랑이야! 그는 무서워! 그가 와서 너를 먹을거야!"

호랑이는 아이가 그를 무서워하기를 원했습니다. 그러나, 아이는 여전히 울었습니다. 호랑이는 실망했습니다.

엄마가 말했습니다. "봐! 감이야!" 아이가 울음을 멈추었습니다.

호랑이는 생각했습니다. '감이 나보다 더 무서워?' 호랑이는 무서워했습니다. 그는 감이 그를 공격하기를 원하지 않았습니다. 그는 도망갔습니다. 그는 다시는 마을로 돌아오지 않았습니다.

❖ ❖ ❖

The Tiger and the Dried Persimmon

❖ *This story is about a foolish tiger who is afraid of a dried persimmon.* ❖

In the mountains there was a small village. There was a tiger in the mountains. One winter evening, the tiger was hungry. He went into the village to find food. He came to a house and stopped outside. A child was crying in the house. The mother tried to stop the crying. The mother said, "Look! A fox! He'll come and eat you!" The child didn't stop crying.

The mother tried again. "Look! A bear! He'll come and eat you!" The child didn't stop crying.

The mother said, "Look! A tiger! He is scary! He will come and eat you!"

The tiger wanted the baby to be afraid of him. However, the child kept crying. The tiger was disappointed.

The mother said, "Look! A persimmon!" The baby stopped crying.

The tiger thought, "The persimmon is scarier than I am?" The tiger was scared. He didn't want the persimmon to attack him. He ran away. He never came back to the village.

❖ ❖ ❖

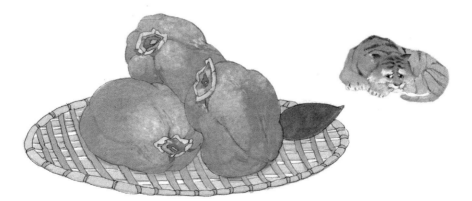

Pre-Reading Questions (answer in Korean or English)

a. 호랑이가 무엇입니까? What is "Horang-i"?

b. 감이 무엇입니까? What is "Gam?"

c. 이 이야기가 무엇에 관한 이야기라고 생각합니까?
   What do you think this story is about?

d. 누가 도망간다고 생각하고 그 이유가 무엇입니까?
   Who is running away in this story and why?

Vocabulary

산 **san** a mountain

작다 **jakda** small

마을 **ma-eul** a village

호랑이 **horang-i** a tiger

겨울 **gyeo-ul** winter

저녁 **jeonyeok** evening

배고프다 **baegopeuda** hungry

찾다 **chatda** to find

음식 **eumsik** food

집 **jip** a house

밖 **bak** outside

아이 **ai** a child

울다 **ulda** to cry

엄마 **eomma** a mother

여우 **yeo-u** a fox

곰 **gom** a bear

먹다 **meokda** to eat

무섭다 **museopda** scary

실망하다 **silmanghada** disappointed

도망가다 **domang-gada** to run away

Culture Notes

Have you tried **gojgam**? **Gojgam** is a dried persimmon after it has been peeled. In ancient times in Korea, fruit was not available in the winter. Due to the lack of sweets at that time, people enjoyed **gojgam** instead. Nowadays, people don't eat as much **gojgam** but during big Korean traditional holidays such as **Chuseok** (Thanksgiving) and **Seollal** (New Year's) it is a must-have.

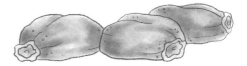

Comprehension Questions

a. 왜 호랑이가 그의 집을 떠났습니까? Why did the tiger leave his house?
b. 호랑이가 무엇을 보고 들었습니까? What did the tiger see and hear?
c. 무엇이 아이를 무섭게 했습니까? What made the child scared?
d. 결국 호랑이는 무엇을 했습니까? In the end, what did the tiger do?

Writing Activity

Write a letter to the tiger from the mother, the baby or the persimmon. What advice do you want to give the tiger or what would you like to say to the tiger?

삼 년 고개

Sam Nyeon Gogae

옛날에, 한 노인이 있었습니다. 그는 한 작은 마을에 살았습니다. 그의 집 옆에 언덕이 있었습니다. 그 언덕에 대한 이야기가 있었습니다. 어떤 사람이 그 언덕에서 넘어지면, 그는 오직 삼 년만 살 수 있었습니다. 그래서, 그 언덕은 삼 년 언덕이라고 불렸습니다. 노인이 그 언덕 위를 걸을 때, 그는 매우 조심했습니다. 어느 날, 그는 그 언덕에서 넘어졌습니다. 그는 매우 슬펐습니다. 그는 삼 년 보다 더 오래 살고 싶었습니다. 그는 침대에 누워서 걱정하고 있었습니다. 한 소년이 그를 방문했습니다.

그 소년이 물었습니다, "왜 슬퍼 보이세요?"

노인이 그에게 무슨 일이 일어났는지 말했습니다. 그 소년은 똑똑했습니다. 그 소년이 말했습니다, "걱정하지 마세요! 해결책이 있어요! 만약 당신이 그 언덕에서 열 번 넘어지면 당신은 30 년을 더 살 수 있을거예요!"

노인은 웃었습니다. 그들은 함께 언덕에 갔습니다. 그들은 언덕에서 굴렀습니다. 그들은 언덕에서 넘어지는 것을 즐겼습니다. 노인은 절대 걱정하지 않았습니다.

❖ ❖ ❖

Three-Years Hill

❖   *This story is about an old man and a wise boy.*   ❖

A long time ago, there was an old man. He lived in a small village. There was a hill next to his house. There was a story about the hill, that if someone fell down the hill, he would live for only three years. So, the hill was called "Three-Years Hill." When the old man walked on the hill, he was always so careful. One day, he fell down the hill. He was so sad. He wanted to live more than three more years. He was lying in bed and worrying, when a little boy visited him.

The boy asked, "Why do you look sad?"

The old man told him what happened. The little boy was wise and said, "Don't worry! There's a solution! If you fall down the hill ten times, you'll live for thirty more years!"

The old man laughed. They went to the hill together. They tumbled down it, enjoying falling down the hill. The old man never worried again.

❖ ❖ ❖

Pre-Reading Questions (answer in Korean or English)

a. 제목을 읽어보세요. 무엇에 관한 이야기일거라고 생각합니까?
    Read the title. What do you think this story is about?

b. 이야기를 빠르게 읽어보세요. 무엇에 관한 이야기일거라고 생각합니까?
    Skim through the story. What do you think this story is about?

c. 당신의 인생에서 누가 가장 현명한 사람입니까?
    Who is the wisest person in your life?

Vocabulary

노인 **no-in** an old man

살다 **salda** to live

작은 마을 **jageun maeul**
  a small village

언덕 **eondeok** a hill

넘어지다 **neomeojida** to fall down

삼 년 **sam nyeon** three years

걷다 **gutda** to walk

조심하다 **josimhada** to be careful

슬프다 **seulpeuda** to be sad

눕다 **nupda** to lay down

침대 **chimdae** a bed

걱정하다 **geokjeonghada** to worry

소년 **sonyeon** a little boy

방문하다 **bangmunhada** to visit

똑똑하다 **ttokttokhada** to be wise

해결책 **haegyeolchaek** a solution

삼 십 **samsip** thirty

웃다 **utda** to laugh

함께 **hamkke** together

즐기다 **jeulgida** to enjoy

절대~않다 **jeoldae~anta** never

Culture Notes

A **gogae** (mountain pass) is the low point between two mountains. Historically, Korean people had to cross many mountain passes to get to different villages. People could not travel to other villages very easily. Because of these many mountain passes, to this day there are many Korean dialects that came about because the people were isolated in distant villages.

Comprehension Questions

a. 삼 년 고개가 무엇입니까? What is the "Three-Years Hill"?
b. 노인에게 무슨 일이 생겼습니까? What happened to the old man?
c. 그 남자는 무엇을 원했습니까? What did the man want?
d. 누가 노인을 방문했습니까? Who visited the old man?
e. 무엇이 그 소년의 해결책이었습니까? What was the little boy's solution?
f. 노인과 소년이 무엇을 했습니까? What did the old man and the little boy do?

Writing Activity

Create a brochure for a vacation spot that adds years to your life (such as a hill that when you rolled down, it will add a year to your life for every certain number of rolls).

혹부리 할아버지

Hogbuli Hal-abeoji

옛날에 목에 혹이 달린 할아버지가 있었습니다. 할아버지는 산에 나무를 하러 갔습니다. 집에 오는 길에 밤이 되었습니다. 할아버지는 무서워서 노래를 불렀습니다. 아름다운 노래를 듣고 도깨비들이 왔습니다. 도깨비들이 할아버지에게 어디에서 그 아름다운 노래가 나오냐고 물었습니다. 할아버지는 혹에서 노래가 나온다고 말했습니다. 도깨비들은 할아버지의 혹을 가져가고 돈을 주었습니다. 할아버지는 부자가 되어 행복하게 살았습니다.

❖ ❖ ❖

The Old Man with the Lump

❖ *This story is about an old man with a lump, and goblins.* ❖

Long ago, there was an old man with a lump on his chin. The old man went to the mountain to cut wood. On his way home, night fell. The old man sang a song because he felt scared. **Dokkabi** heard a beautiful song and came to the old man. **Dokkabi** asked where the beautiful song was coming from. The old man answered that it came out of his lump. **Dokkabi** took the lump away from him and gave him a lot of money. The old man became rich and lived happily ever after.

❖ ❖ ❖

Pre-Reading Questions (answer in Korean or English)

a. 혹부리가 무엇입니까? What is a **Hokburi**?
b. 무서울 때 노래를 부른 적이 있습니까?
   Have you ever sung when you were scared?
c. 도깨비가 나오는 이야기를 들어 본 적이 있습니까?
   Have you ever heard a story about **Dokkabi**?

Vocabulary

혹부리 **hokburi** a person with a lump
할아버지 **hal-abeoji** an old man
목 **mok** neck
혹 **hok** a lump
산 **san** a mountain
나무를 하다 **namuleul hada**
   to cut wood
집에 오는 길 **jip-e o-neon gil**
   on one's way home
밤 **bam** night
무섭다 **museopda** scary

노래를 부르다 **noraeleul buleuda**
   to sing
오다 **oda** to come
아름답다 **areumdapda** beautiful
도깨비 **dokkabi** a goblin
어디 **eodi** where
나오다 **naoda** to come out
가져가다 **gajeogada** to take away
돈 **don** money
부자 **buja** a rich person
행복하다 **haeng-bokhada** to be happy
살다 **salda** to live

Culture Notes

This story is one of the best-known Korean folktales outside of Korea. There are similar folktales in Japanese and other languages. The tale is meant to warn against selfish deception and cunning.

Comprehension Questions

a. 할아버지는 왜 노래를 불렀습니까? Why did the old man sing a song?
b. 도깨비들은 왜 할아버지에게 왔습니까?
   Why did **Dokkabi** come to the old man?
c. 할아버지는 노래가 어디에서 나온다고 했습니까?
   Where did the old man say his song came from?
d. 도깨비들은 할아버지에게서 무엇을 가져가고 할아버지에게 무엇을 주었습니까? What did **Dokkabi** take away from the old man, and what did he give him?

Writing Activity

Write a few sentences about how the old man could be happy (even though he lied). Discuss it with your classmates.

금덩이를 버린 형제

Geumdeong ileul Beolin Hyeongje

옛날에 두 형제가 있었습니다. 그들은 서로 좋아했습니다. 어느 날 그들은 다리 위를 걷고 있었습니다. 남동생이 물 속에서 금 두 덩이를 찾았습니다. 그가 금 한 덩이를 그의 형에게 주었습니다. 그들이 배를 탔습니다. 남동생이 갑자기 그의 금덩이를 바다 속으로 던졌습니다. 그가 말했습니다, "나는 형의 금을 훔치는 것에 대해서 생각했어. 금이 나를 욕심이 많게 만들었어." 형은 그의 남동생을 자랑스러워했습니다. 그 또한 그의 금을 물 속으로 던졌습니다.

❖ ❖ ❖

Two Brothers Who Threw Away
Their Lumps of Gold

❖ *This story is about two good brothers who love each other.* ❖

A long time ago, there were two brothers. They liked each other. One day, they were walking on a bridge. The younger brother found two lumps of gold in the water. He gave a lump of gold to his older brother. They went on a boat. The younger brother suddenly threw his lump of gold into the water. He said, "I thought about stealing your gold. The gold has made me greedy." The older brother was proud of his younger brother. He also threw his gold into the water.

❖ ❖ ❖

Pre-Reading Questions (answer in Korean or English)

a. 제목과 단어를 보세요. 등장인물들에 대해 어떤 것을 추측할 수 있습니까?
   Read the title. What can you assume about the characters?
b. 이야기가 어디에서 발생했다고 생각하십니까?
   Where do you think the story happened?
c. 이야기에서 어떤일이 발생했다고 생각하십니까?
   What do you think happened in the story?

Vocabulary

옛날에 **yetnal-e** a long time ago
두- **du** two
형제 **hyeongje** brothers
서로 좋아하다 **seoro joahada**
   to like each other
남동생 **namdongsaeng** a younger
   brother
찾다 **chatta** to find
덩이 **deong-i** lumps
금 **geum** gold
물 **mul** water
주다 **juda** to give

형 **hyeong** an older brother
배 **bae** a boat
갑자기 **gabjagi** suddenly
던지다 **deonjida** to throw
~속으로 **sok euro** into
~에 대해 생각하다 **e daehae
   saenggakhada** to think about
훔치다 **humchida** to steal
욕심이 많다 **yoksimi manta** to be
   greedy
자랑스럽다 **jarang seureobda**
   to be proud

Culture Notes

There are many Korean traditional folktales that teach about sibling love and respect. In these stories, characters turn out well when they have good sibling relationships. On the other hand, a person who is hateful and mean to another sibling gets punished. Through such stories, we learn that we should be good to our siblings. This story is a representative one that gives a good example of brothers who love each other.

Comprehension Questions

a. 형제들이 서로에 대해 어떻게 생각했습니까?
   How did the brothers think about each other?
b. 남동생이 무엇을 찾았습니까? What did the younger brother find?
c. 왜 남동생이 금을 바다속에 던졌습니까?
   Why did the younger brother throw the gold into the sea?
d. 형이 무엇을 했습니까? What did the older brother do?

Writing Activity

Write about someone who you love enough to share gold with, and then throw it away to protect the relationship.

금도끼와 은도끼

Geumdokkiwa Eundokki

　옛날에 두 명의 친구들이 있었습니다. 그들의 이름은 덕보와 윤보였습니다. 덕보는 착했습니다. 윤보는 게으르고 욕심이 많았습니다. 어느 날, 덕보가 산에 올라갔습니다. 그는 나무를 베었습니다. 그가 그의 도끼를 떨어뜨렸습니다. 그의 도끼는 연못에 빠졌습니다. 덕보는 울었습니다. 산신령이 연못으로부터 나왔습니다. 그가 덕보에게 금도끼가 그의 도끼인지 물었습니다. 덕보는 아니라고 했습니다. 산신령이 은도끼가 그의 도끼인지 물었습니다. 덕보는 아니라고 했습니다. 덕보가 그의 도끼는 쇠도끼라고 했습니다. 덕보는 정직했습니다. 산신령은 그의 정직함을 좋아했습니다. 그가 덕보에게 금도끼, 은도끼, 쇠도끼를 주었습니다. 윤보는 질투했습니다. 그가 산에 올라갔습니다. 그는 도끼를 연못에 떨어뜨렸습니다. 산신령이 나왔습니다. 그가 윤보에게 금도끼가 그의 도끼인지 물었습니다. 윤보가 그렇다고 했습니다. 산신령은 화가 났습니다. 윤보는 아무 도끼도 받지 못했습니다. 그 대신에 산신령은 그의 머리를 쳤습니다.

❖ ❖ ❖

The Golden Ax and the Silver Ax

❖   *This story is about one honest man and one greedy man.*   ❖

A long time ago, there were two friends. Their names were Deokbo and Yun-bo. Deokbo was kind. Yunbo was lazy and greedy. One day, Deokbo went up a mountain. He was cutting wood. He dropped his ax. His ax fell into a pond. Deokbo cried. A Mountain God came out of the pond. He asked Deokbo if his ax was gold. Deokbo said, "No." The Mountain God asked if his ax was silver. Deokbo said, "No." Deokbo said his ax was an iron ax. Deokbo was honest. The Mountain God liked his honesty. He gave Deokbo a gold, silver, and iron ax. Yunbo was jealous. He went up to the mountain. He dropped his ax in the pond. A Mountain God came out. He asked Yunbo if his ax was gold. Yunbo said, "Yes." The Mountain God was mad. Yunbo received no ax. The Mountain God gave him a hit on the head instead.

❖ ❖ ❖

Pre-Reading Questions (answer in Korean or English)

a. 정직함이란 무엇입니까? What is honesty?

b. 정직함은 언제 중요합니까? Why is honesty important?

c. 정직한 사람이 언제나 승리합니까? Do honest people always win?

d. 이 이야기가 무엇에 관한 이야기라고 생각하나요?
   What do you think this story is about?

Vocabulary

둘 **dul** two

친구들 **chin-gu-deul** friends

게으르다 **ge-eu-reuda** lazy

욕심이 많다 **yoksimimanta** greedy

산 **san** a mountain

자르다/베다 **jareuda/beda** to cut

나무 **namu** wood

떨어뜨리다 **tteoreotteurida** to drop

빠지다 **ppajida** to fall

연못 **yeonmot** a pond

신 **shin** a god

은 **eun** silver

금 **geum** gold

쇠 **soe** iron

정직함 **jeongjikham** honesty

질투하다 **jiltuhada** jealous

화가 나다 **hwaganada** mad

받다 **batta** to receive

치다 **chida** to hit

머리 **meori** head

Culture Notes

In olden times, the Korean people believed that there was a guardian spirit of mountains called **Sansinreung** (the Mountain God). In Korean traditional fairytales, the Mountain God sometimes appeared in the shape of a human. At other times, it appeared in the shape of a tiger. Since people believed that the Mountain God protected the country, they prayed to him for help when there was a concern, problem, or disaster within the country. Shrines where people prayed to the Mountain God can be found in Buddhist temples in Korea today.

Comprehension Questions

a. 윤보는 어떤 사람이었나요? What was Yunbo like?

b. 덕보는 어떤 사람이었나요? What was Deokbo like?

c. 덕보가 어디로 갔습니까? Where did Deokbo go?

d. 덕보가 무엇을 했습니까? What did Deokbo do?

c. 덕보는 정직했나요? Was Deokbo honest?

f. 무엇이 연못에 떨어졌나요? What fell into the pond?

g. 산신령이 덕보에게 무엇을 주었습니까?
   What did the Mountain God give to Deokbo?

h. 산신령이 윤보에게 무엇을 주었습니까?
   What did the Mountain God give to Yunbo?

Writing Activity

Write a short paragraph about the kind of person you are. Are you more like Deokbo or are you more like Yunbo? Are there appropriate times to act like each of the characters, or not? How has your honesty—or lack of honesty—served you in your life?

흥부와 놀부

Heungbuwa Nolbu

옛날에 두 형제가 있었습니다. 그들의 이름은 흥부와 놀부였습니다. 놀부는 많은 돈이 있었습니다. 그는 욕심이 많았습니다. 흥부는 돈이 없었습니다. 그는 관대했습니다. 어느 날, 흥부가 새 한 마리를 찾았습니다. 그 새는 부러진 다리를 가졌습니다. 그는 그 새를 도와 주었습니다. 그는 새를 그의 집으로 데려갔습니다. 새는 나았습니다.

그는 날아갔습니다. 나중에 그 새가 흥부에게 세 개의 씨를 주었습니다. 박이 한 개 자랐습니다. 그것은 매우 컸습니다. 흥부는 그것을 잘랐습니다. 금화가 나왔습니다. 놀부 또한 그 금화를 원했습니다. 그가 새를 발견했습니다. 그가 그 새의 다리를 부러뜨렸습니다. 새가 도망갔습니다. 나중에 그 새가 놀부에게 세 개의 씨를 가져다 주었습니다. 박이 한 개 자랐습니다. 놀부는 그것을 잘랐습니다. 악마가 나왔습니다! 그 악마가 놀부를 때렸습니다. 놀부는 욕심이 많은 것은 좋지 않다는 것을 배웠습니다.

❖ ❖ ❖

Heungboo and Nolbu

❖ *This is a story about two brothers. One is greedy and the other is generous.* ❖

A long time ago there were two brothers. Their names were Heungboo and Nolbu. Nolbu had lots of money. He was greedy. Heungboo had no money. He was generous. One day, Heungboo found a bird. The bird had a broken leg. He helped the bird. He took the bird to his house. The bird got better. It flew away. Later the bird brought three seeds to Heungboo. A gourd grew. It was very big. Heungboo cut it open. Gold coins came out.

Nolbu also wanted gold coins. He found a bird. He broke the bird's leg. The bird ran away. Later the bird brought three seeds to Nolbu. A gourd grew. Nolbu cut it open. A devil came out! The devil hit Nolbu. Nolbu learned that greed is not good.

❖ ❖ ❖

Pre-Reading Questions (answer in Korean or English)

a. 욕심이란 무엇입니까? What is greed?

b. 욕심이 많은 사람을 아십니까? 설명해보세요.
   Do you know a greedy person? Please explain.

c. 이 이야기에서 무엇이 일어난다고 생각하십니까?
   What do you think will happen in the story?

Vocabulary

형제 **hyeongje** brothers

돈 **don** money

욕심 **yoksim** greedy

관대 **gwandae** generous

새 **sae** bird

부러진 다리 **bureojin dari** a broken
   leg

돕다 **dopda** to help

집 **jip** a house

낫다 **natta** to get better

날아가다 **naragada** to fly away

세 **se** three

씨앗 **ssiat** seeds

금화 **geumhwa** gold coins

도망가다 **domanggada** to run away

자르다 **jareuda** to cut open

악마 **akma** devil

Culture Notes

One popular Korean proverb goes "**jebido eunhyeleul gapneunda**" (or "Even a swallow returns a favor" in English). This proverb refers to the idea that it is important for everyone to return a favor, whether one is rich or poor, big or small. In the story "Heungboo and Nolbu" we learn that virtue and goodness are rewarded and evil is punished. The story also points out that in the end, justice will prevail, and that the love and care that we have for others, especially for our siblings, is a key to our happiness.

Comprehension Questions

a. 형제가 몇 명 있습니까? How many brothers are there in this story?

b. 누가 욕심이 많습니까? Who is the greedy one?

c. 새가 흥부에게 무엇을 가져다 주었습니까?
   What did the bird bring to Heungboo?

d. 놀부의 박에는 무엇이 있었습니까? What was the thing in Nolbu's gourd?

Writing Activity

Rewrite the ending (in English or Korean). What do you think came out of Nolbu's gourd? What happened to Nolbu after that? Read your ending to the class or draw a picture of it on the board and explain it in Korean.

견우와 직녀

Gyeon-uhwa Jignyeo

옛날에 한 공주가 있었습니다. 그녀는 하늘에서 살았습니다. 그 공주의 이름은 직녀였습니다. 그녀는 한 농부를 좋아했습니다. 그의 이름은 견우였습니다. 왕이 그들의 관계를 좋아하지 않았습니다. 그러나 견우와 직녀는 서로를 좋아했습니다. 그 왕은 화가 났습니다. 그가 그들을 떨어뜨렸습니다. 그가 견우를 동쪽으로 보냈고, 직녀를 서쪽으로 보냈습니다. 그래서 그들은 서로를 볼 수가 없었습니다. 그들은 매일 울었습니다. 왕은 안타까워했습니다. 왕이 그들에게 일년에 한 번씩 만나도록 허락해 주었습니다. 까마귀 떼와 까치 떼가 그들을 도왔습니다. 까마귀 떼와 까치 떼가 그들을 위해 다리를 만들었습니다. 견우와 직녀는 매년 다리 위에서 울었습니다. 그들의 눈물이 비가 되었습니다.

❖ ❖ ❖

The Story of Gyeon-Uh and Jik-Nyeo

❖   *This story is about a loving couple who can only meet once a year.*   ❖

A long time ago, there was a princess. She lived in heaven. The princess's name was Jik-Nyeo. She liked a farmer. His name was Gyeon-Uh. The king didn't like their relationship, but Gyeon-Uh and Jik-Nyeo liked each other. The king was mad. He separated them. He sent Gyeon-Uh to the east and sent Jik-Nyeo to the west so they couldn't see each other. They cried every day. The king felt sorry. The king allowed them to meet once a year. Crows and magpies helped them by making a bridge for them. Gyeon-Uh and Jik-Nyeo cried on the bridge year after year. Their tears became rain.

❖ ❖ ❖

Pre-Reading Questions (answer in Korean or English)

a. 단어들을 보십시오. 이 이야기는 무엇에 관한 이야기입니까?
   Look at the words. What is the story about?
b. '금지된 사랑'이란 무엇입니까? What is "forbidden love"?
c. 공주가 농부와 결혼할 수 있습니까? Can a princess marry a farmer?
d. 그들이 좋은 부부생활을 할 수 있습니까? Can they be a good couple?

Vocabulary

공주 **gongju** a princess
하늘 **haneul** heaven
이름 **ireum** name
농부 **nongbu** a farmer
왕 **wang** a king
좋아하지 않다 **joahaji anta** to not like
관계 **gwangye** relationship
좋아하다 **joahada** to like
서로 **seoro** each other
화가 나다 **hwaganada** to be mad
떨어뜨리다 **tteoreotteurida**
   to separate
동쪽 **dongjjok** east
서쪽 **seojjok** west

보다 **boda** to see
울다 **ulda** to cry
매일 **maeil** every day
안타까워 하다 **antakkawo hada**
   to feel sorry
허락하다 **heorakhada** to allow
만나다 **man-nada** to meet
일 년에 한 번 **il nyeone hanbeon**
   once a year
까마귀 떼 **kkamagui tte** crows
까치 떼 **kkachi tte** magpies
도와주다 **dowajuda** to help
다리 **dari** a bridge
비 **bi** rain

Culture Notes

Gyeon-Uh and Jik-Nyeo could only meet once a year, on 7 July according to the lunar calendar (a day called **Chil-weol-chil-seok**). In the old days, it was important for Korean women to be good at sewing and to be able to give birth to baby boys. Therefore, on 7 July they always prayed to Jik-Nyeo to be blessed in those two things. If it happened to rain on 7 July, Koreans believed the rain represented the tears of happiness because Gyeon-Uh had met Jik-Nyeo.

Comprehension Questions

a. 직녀가 어디에 살았습니까? Where did Jik-Nyeo live?

b. 견우가 누구입니까? Who was Gyeon-Uh?

c. 왜 왕은 그들의 관계를 좋아하지 않았습니까?
   Why did the king not approve of their relationship?

d. 왕이 견우를 어디로 보냈습니까? 그가 직녀를 어디에 보냈습니까?
   Where did the king send Gyeon-Uh? Where did he send Jik-Nyeo?

e. 어떻게 까마귀와 까치가 그들을 만나도록 도왔습니까?
   How did crows and magpies help them to meet?

f. 그들의 눈물이 무엇이 되었습니까?
   What happened to their tears?

Writing Activity

Read the story, and then create a storyboard or write a few sentences showing what you think happened next.

바보 온달과 평강공주

Babo Ondalgwa Pyeong-gang-gongju

옛날에 한 남자가 있었고, 그의 이름은 온달이였습니다. 사람들은 그를 바보라고 생각했습니다. 사람들은 그를 "바보 온달"이라고 불렀습니다. 한 공주가 있었습니다. 그녀의 이름은 평강이였습니다. 그녀는 자주 울었습니다. 그녀의 아버지는 그녀에게 울지 말라고 했습니다. 만약 그녀가 울면, 그녀는 바보 온달과 결혼해야 했습니다. 평강공주는 어른이 되었습니다. 그녀의 아버지는 똑똑한 사위를 원했습니다. 그러나 평강은 바보 온달과 결혼하기를 원했습니다. 그녀의 아버지는 화가 났습니다. 그래서, 그는 그녀를 쫓아냈습니다. 평강은 온달의 집에 갔습니다. 평강과 온달은 결혼했습니다. 평강은 그에게 많은 것을 가르쳤습니다. 그는 양궁과 문학을 배웠습니다. 이웃 나라가 그들의 나라를 침략했습니다. 사람들이 도망갔습니다. 그러나 온달은 도망가지 않았습니다. 그는 적과 싸웠습니다. 그는 적의 장군을 죽였습니다. 사람들이 온달을 칭찬했습니다. 왕이 온달에게 상을 주었습니다.

❖ ❖ ❖

Stupid On-Dal and Princess Pyeong-Gang

❖ *This story is about a smart princess who turns a stupid boy into a man.* ❖

A long time ago, there was a man whose name was On-Dal. People thought that he was stupid, so they called him "Stupid On-Dal." There was a little princess. Her name was Pyeong-Gang. She often cried. Her father told her to stop crying, because if she cried she would marry Stupid On-Dal. The princess Pyeong-Gang became an adult. Her father wanted a smart son-in-law, but Pyeong-Gang wanted to marry Stupid On-Dal. Her father became mad, so he kicked her out. Pyeong-Gang went to On-Dal's house and they got married. Pyeong-Gang taught him many things. He learned archery and literature. A neighboring country invaded their country. People ran away. But On-Dal did not run away. He fought against the enemy. He killed the enemy's general. People praised On-Dal. Afterward, the king rewarded him.

❖ ❖ ❖

Pre-Reading Questions (answer in Korean or English)

a. 무엇이 똑똑한 사람을 만듭니까? What makes a smart person?

b. 우리는 왜 다른 사람을 바보라고 부릅니까? Why do we call someone a fool?

c. 어떤 유형의 친구를 좋아합니까? What kind of friends do you like?

Vocabulary

남자 **namja** a man

이름 **ireum** a name

사람들 **saramdeul** people

생각하다 **saenggakhada** to think

바보 **babo** a stupid person

작은 **jag-eun** little

공주 **gongju** a princess

울다 **ulda** to cry

결혼하다 **gyeolhonhada** to marry

되다 **doeda** to become

어른 **orun** an adult

똑똑하다 **ttokttokhada** smart

원하다 **wonhada** to want

화가 나다 **hwaganada** to be mad

쫓아내다 **jjocha-naeda** to kick out

배우다 **bae-u-da** to learn

양궁 **yanggoong** archery

문학 **munhak** literature

이웃 나라 **i-ut-nara** neighboring country

침략하다 **chimryakhada** to invade

도망가다 **domanggada** to run away

죽이다 **jugida** to kill

칭찬하다 **chingchanhada** to praise

상을 주다 **sang-euljuda** to reward

Culture Notes

Unlike Princess Pyeong-Gang, On-Dal was a commoner and not an aristocrat. It was impossible for a princess to marry a commoner in the old days. The story "Stupid On-Dal and Princess Pyeong-Gang" shows that love can overcome all social boundaries. In the postscript to this story, Stupid On-Dal became a general and died on the battlefield. When later on his soldiers tried to move his coffin, it would not budge one bit. It was as if the coffin were waiting for someone. It was only after Princess Pyeong-Gang came and said, "Let's go home" that the soldiers were finally able to move the coffin.

Comprehension Questions

a. 온달이 누구입니까? Who is On-Dal?

b. 공주의 이름이 무엇입니까? What is the princess's name?

c. 왜 공주의 아버지는 공주가 온달과 결혼하는 것을 원하지 않았습니까?
   Why did the princess's father not want her to marry On-Dal?

d. 공주가 온달과 결혼했습니까? Did the princess marry On-Dal?

e. 이 이야기에서 진짜 바보는 누구입니까? Who is the actual fool in this story?

Writing Activity

Before you read the story, skim the title and the vocabulary words. Write a few sentences addressing what you think the story will be about.

소가 된 게으름뱅이

Soga Doen Geeuleumbaeng-i

한 소년이 있었습니다. 그는 일하기를 싫어했습니다. 그는 누워서 하루종일 낮잠자기를 좋아했습니다. 사람들이 그를 '게으름뱅이'라고 불렀습니다. 그는 심지어 그의 침대에서 저녁 먹기를 좋아했습니다. 그의 어머니가 말했습니다, "먹은 후에 눕는 것은 좋지 않아." 그녀는 그가 소가 될 것이라고 말했습니다. 그는 신경쓰지 않았습니다. 그는 소가 되고 싶었습니다. 소들은 어느 때에나 잘 수 있습니다. 그것은 좋은 것입니다. 한 노인이 그를 방문했습니다. 그 노인은 그에게 소 가면을 주었습니다. 그 가면에는 마법이 걸려 있었습니다. 그 소 가면은 그를 소로 만들 수 있었습니다. 그가 그 가면을 썼습니다. 그가 소가 되었습니다. 그는 흥분했습니다. 그는 하루 종일 낮잠을 자고 싶었습니다. 그러나, 사람들은 그를 채찍질했습니다. 그들은 그가 하루 종일 일하도록 만들었습니다. 그것은 힘들고 고통스러웠습니다. 그는 매일 일했습니다. 그가 그의 어머니를 그리워했습니다. 그가 넘어졌습니다. 그가 후회했습니다. 그러더니 그가 그의 눈을 떴습니다. 그것은 꿈이었습니다. 그것은 단지 악몽이었습니다. 그 날 이후에, 그의 인생은 변화했습니다. 그 소년은 부지런해졌고, 어머니의 말씀을 잘 들었습니다.

❖ ❖ ❖

54

The Lazy Boy Who Became a Cow

✤ *This story is about a really lazy boy.* ✤

There was a boy. He hated work. He liked to lie down and take naps all day. People called him "lazy." He even liked to eat dinner in his bed. His mother said, "It is not good to lie down after eating." She said he would become a cow. He didn't care. He wanted to be a cow. Cows can sleep any time—that is good! An old man visited him. The old man gave him a cow mask. The cow mask was magical. The cow mask could make him a cow. He wore the mask and became a cow. He was excited. He wanted to take a nap all day, but people whipped him. They made him work all day. It was hard and painful. He worked every day. He missed his mother. He fell down. He had regrets. Then he opened his eyes. It was a dream. It was just a bad dream. After that day, his life changed. The boy became diligent and listened to his mother.

✤ ✤ ✤

Pre-Reading Questions (answer in Korean or English)

a. 나이가 들면 무엇이 되고 싶은가요?

   What do you want to be when you get older?

b. 제일 쉬운 직업이 무엇입니까? 제일 힘든 직업은 무엇입니까?

   What is the easiest job? What is your most difficult job?

c. 무엇을 후회합니까? What do you regret?

Vocabulary

소년 **sonyeon** a boy

싫어하다 **sireohada** to hate

일하다 **ilhada** to work

눕다 **nupda** to lay down

사람들 **saramdeul** people

게으르다 **ge-eu-reuda** lazy

먹다 **meokda** to eat

저녁 **jeo-nyeok** dinner

침대 **chimdae** a bed

소 **so** a cow

신경쓰다 **shin-gyeong sseuda** to care

자다 **jada** to sleep

노인 **noin** an old man

방문하다 **bangmunhada** to visit

가면 **gamyeon** a mask

마법이 걸린 **mabeobi itneun** magical

쓰다 **sseuda** to wear (a mask)

흥분하다 **heungbunhada** to be excited

힘들다 **himdeulda** to be hard

고통스럽다 **gotong seu-reobda** to be painful

그리워하다 **geuriwohada** to miss

채찍질하다 **chaejjikjilhada** to whip

꿈을 꾸다 **kkumulkkuda** to dream

후회하다 **hu-hwehada** to regret

변하다 **byeonhada** to change

부지런하다 **bujireonhada** to be diligent

듣다 **deutta** to listen

Culture Notes

In Korea there are sayings such as, "You'll turn into a cow if you lie down right after eating" and "You'll turn into a cow if you eat while lying down." Why would one think that a lazy person would become a cow? Historically, cows diligently helped Koreans with farming. Koreans believe that such sayings would encourage the lazy to learn diligence and become earnest from the example of cows, who were such hard workers.

Comprehension Questions

a. 소년이 무엇을 하기를 좋아했습니까? What did the boy like to do?

b. 소년이 어디에서 저녁을 먹었습니까? Where did the boy eat dinner?

c. 어머니는 왜 소년이 소가 될 것이라고 했습니까?
   Why did the mother say that the boy would be a cow?

d. 소년은 무엇이 되고 싶었습니까? What did the boy want to be?

e. 소년은 소가 된 것을 좋아했습니까? 그 이유는 무엇입니까?
   Did the boy like to be a cow? Why?

Writing Activity

Write a short paragraph about an animal you would like to be. Why would you like to be that animal?

사람으로 둔갑한 쥐

Salam-eulo Dungabhan Jwi

옛날 옛날에 한 사람이 산 속에서 공부를 하고 있었습니다. 산 속에는 아무도 없어서 아주 외로웠습니다. 어느 날, 쥐 한 마리가 매일 놀러 오기 시작했습니다. 그 사람이 쥐에게 음식을 주었지만 먹지 않았습니다. 그래서 손톱을 주었더니 쥐가 손톱을 먹었습니다. 그 사람은 계속 쥐에게 손톱을 주었습니다. 어느 날 갑자기, 쥐가 오지 않았습니다. 그 사람은 계속 기다렸습니다. 하지만 쥐는 계속 오지 않았습니다. 그 사람은 조금 섭섭했지만 다시 공부를 시작했습니다.

공부를 다 하고 집으로 돌아갔는데, 그 사람과 똑같이 생긴 사람이 집에 있었습니다. 그 사람은 놀랐습니다. 가족들은 그 사람이 가짜라고 생각해서 내쫓았습니다. 그 사람은 슬퍼서 기도했습니다. 그 사람의 꿈에 할아버지가 나와서 고양이를 집에 데려가라고 했습니다. 그 사람은 고양이를 데리고 집에 가서 가짜에게 던졌습니다. 고양이가 가짜를 물어뜯으니까 가짜가 쥐로 변했습니다. 그 사람은 가족들과 다시 행복하게 잘 살았습니다.

The Mouse in the Shape of a Man

❖   *This story is about a lonely man and a mouse.*   ❖

Once upon a time, there was a man who was studying on a mountain. Because there was no one else on the mountain, he was really lonely. One day, a mouse came and visited him. The man gave food to the mouse, but the mouse did not eat it. Then the man gave the mouse his fingernail trimmings, and the mouse ate them. Day after day, the man kept giving trimmed fingernails to the mouse. One day, suddenly, the mouse stopped coming. The man kept waiting, day after day, but the mouse never came. The man was sad for a little, but he started to study again. When he finished studying, he went back home. When he arrived, there was a person who looked exactly like himself at his house already. The man was surprised. The family members threw him out because they thought he was a fake. The man was sad and decided to pray. His grandfather appeared to him in his dream and he told the man to bring a cat to his home. The man went home with a cat and threw the cat at the identical man who was there. The cat bit the imposter, and the imposter was changed back into the mouse. The man then lived with his family happily ever after.

❖ ❖ ❖

Pre-Reading Questions (answer in Korean or English)

a. 어떤 사건이 설명되거나 묘사될 것이라고 생각합니까?

What event do you think is being explained or described?

b. 전래동화에서 쥐의 공통적인 성격은 무엇입니까?

What are some common characteristics that mice have in folktales?

c. 이 이야기에 나오는 쥐의 성격을 추측할 수 있습니까?

What characteristics do you think the mouse will have in this story?

Vocabulary

옛날 옛날에 **yesnal yesnal-e** once upon a time

사람 **salam** a man

공부 **gongbu** to study

아무도 없다 **amudo eobsda** there is no one

아주 **aju** really/very

외롭다 **oelobda** to be lonely

어느 날 **eoneu nal** one day

쥐 **jwi** a mouse

마리 **mali** counters for animals

놀러 오다 **nolleo oda** to visit (lit., to come to)

음식 **eumsig** food

손톱 **sontob** a fingernail

갑자기 **gabjagi** suddenly

계속 **gyesog** to keep

기다리다 **gidalida** to wait

섭섭하다 **seobseobhada** to be sad/disappointed

돌아가다 **dol-agada** to go back/return

똑같이 생기다 **ttoggat-i saeng-gi-da** to look the same

놀라다 **nollada** to be surprised

가족 **gajog** family

~들 **deul** plural for nouns

가짜 **gajja** an imposter/a fake

내쫓다 **naejjochda** to throw someone out

기도하다 **gidohada** to pray

고양이 **goyang-i** a cat

물어뜯다 **mul-eotteudda** to bite

변하다 **byeonhada** to be changed

Culture Notes

In this story, a mouse turns into a human by eating a person's fingernails. In Korea, there is a belief that we should cherish our bodies because they were given to us by our parents. Since things like hair, or fingernails and toenails were a gift from our parents, they should not be thrown away carelessly. "The Mouse in the Shape of a Man" is a fable which shows there will be bad consequences if someone does so.

Comprehension Questions

a. 이 이야기에서 쥐가 어떻게 남자로 바뀌었습니까?

How was the mouse changed into the man in the story?

b. 남자는 어떻게 자신의 상황에 대한 해답을 찾았습니까? 그 해답은 무엇이었습니까?

How did the man find a solution for his situation and what was it?

c. 이 이야기에서 쥐의 성격은 어떻습니까? 이전에 생각했던 것과 어떻게 비슷하거나 다릅니까?

What are the characteristics of the mouse in this story? How are they similar or different from what you previously thought?

Writing Activity

당신이 이 이야기의 남자라면, 이 남자의 상황을 어떻게 해결할지에 대해 짧은 이야기를 쓰세요.

Write a short story about how you would deal with this man's situation, if you were him.

반쪽 아들

Banjjog Adeul

옛날 옛날에 한 부부가 살고 있었습니다. 부부는 나이가 아주 많았지만, 아직 자식이 없었습니다. 그래서 산에 가서 백 일 동안 기도를 하고 아들을 하나 낳았습니다. 하지만 아들은 눈도 하나, 귀도 하나, 팔도 하나, 다리도 하나인 반쪽이었습니다. 하지만 부부는 아들을 아주 사랑하며 키웠습니다. 반쪽 아들은 눈도 하나, 귀도 하나, 팔도 하나, 다리도 하나였지만 신기한 능력이 있었습니다.

어느 날, 반쪽 아들이 어머니에게 물었습니다. "어머니, 우물이 너무 머니까 앞마당에 우물을 하나 팔까요?"

어머니는 대답했습니다. "애야, 너는 팔도 하나고 다리도 하나인데 우물을 어떻게 파니?"

반쪽 아들이 버드나무 가지를 잘라 앞마당에 꽂으니 우물이 생겼습니다. 어머니는 깜짝 놀랐습니다.

또 어느날, 반쪽 아들이 아버지에게 물었습니다. "아버지, 저녁마다 놀 수 있게 앞마당에 바위 하나 가져다 놓을까요?"

아버지는 대답했습니다. "애야, 너는 팔도 하나고 다리도 하나인데 바위를 어떻게 가져다 놓니?"

반쪽 아들은 큰 바위를 번쩍 들어 앞마당에 가져다 놓았습니다. 아버지는 깜짝 놀랐습니다.

어느 날, 반쪽 아들이 한 여자와 결혼하고 싶다고 말했습니다. 반쪽 아들의 부모님이 그 여자의 집에 가서 물어 봤지만, 그 여자의 부모님이 반쪽 아들과는 결혼을 시킬 수 없다고 했습니다.

그날 밤, 반쪽 아들은 밤에 몰래 그 여자의 집에 갔습니다. 반쪽 아들은 그 여자의 부모님의 손을 서로 묶어놓고 소리쳤습니다. "반쪽 아들이 딸을 데려갑니다!"

그 여자의 부모님은 깜짝 놀라 일어나서 반쪽아들을 잡으려고 했습니다. 하지만, 손이 묶여 있는데 서로 반대 쪽으로 가려고 해서 움직일 수 없었습니다. 반쪽 아들은 그 여자를 데리고 집으로 왔습니다. 하룻밤 자고 나서, 반쪽 아들은 눈도 두 개, 귀도 두 개, 팔도 두 개, 다리도 두 개인 아주 잘생긴 남자가 되었습니다.

❖ ❖ ❖

The Half Son

❖ *This story is about a love that made a person whole.* ❖

Once upon a time, there was a married couple. They were very old, but they did not have any children. Therefore, they went to the mountain and prayed for 100 days. After that, they had a son. However, the son was a half son who had only one eye, one ear, one arm, and one leg. The married couple raised the son and loved him very much. Even though the half son had only one eye, one ear, one arm, and one leg, he had miraculous power.

One day, the half son asked his mother, "Mother, because the well is too far, shall I dig a well in the front yard?"

The mother answered, "Dear, you have only one arm and one leg, how can you dig a well?"

The half son cut a branch off a willow tree and stuck it in the front yard, and a well formed. The mother was very surprised.

On another day, the half son asked his father, "Father, for us to be able to play every evening, shall I bring a big rock in the front yard?" The father answered. "Dear, you have only one arm and one leg, how can you bring a rock?" The half son lifted the big rock in an instant and brought it in the front yard. The father was surprised. One day, the half son said that he wanted to marry a girl. His parents visited the girl's house and asked the girl's parents. However, the girl's parents said that she could not marry the half son. That night, the half son secretly went to the girl's house. The half son tied her parents' hands together and yelled out, "This half son will take your daughter!" Her parents woke up startled, and tried to capture the half son. However, because their hands were tied, and they wanted to go in different directions, they could not move. The half son took the daughter and went home. After only one night, the half son became a very handsome man who had two eyes, two ears, two arms, and two legs.

❖ ❖ ❖

Pre-Reading Questions (answer in Korean or English)
a. 어떤 사건이 설명되거나 묘사될 것이라고 생각합니까?
   What event do you think is being explained or described?
b. 제목을 보고 이야기의 의미를 추측할 수 있습니까?
   Based on the title, what do you think the meaning of the story is?

Vocabulary

부부 **bubu** a married couple

나이가 많다 **naiga manta** to be old

자식 **jasig** children

백일 동안 **baeg-il dong-an** for 100 days

아들 **adeul** a son

낳다 **nata** to give birth

눈 **nun** an eye

귀 **gwi** an ear

팔 **pal** an arm

다리 **dali** a leg

반쪽 **banjjog** half (side)

신기하다 **sin-gihada** miraculous

능력 **neunglyeog** power

우물 **umul** a well

파다 **pada** to dig

버드나무 **beodeunamu** a willow tree

바위 **bawi** a rock

앞마당 **ammadang** a front yard

번쩍 들다 **beonjjeog deulda** to lift something easily

결혼 **gyeolhon** marriage

부모님 **bumonim** parents

몰래 **mollae** secretly

묶다 **mukkda** to tie

소리치다 **solichida** to yell out

데려가다 **delyeogada** to bring (a person)

반대쪽 **bandaejjog** opposite side

하룻밤 **halubbam** one night

Culture Notes

In the story, "The Half Son," the parents pray for a hundred days and give birth to only half a son. In Korea, people used to pray for a hundred days when they heartily wished for something. They usually prayed to the guardian spirits of the mountains or to their ancestors. Nowadays, parents pray for a hundred days for good results on important exams, such as the *Su-Neung* test, which is similar to college entrance exams in the United States.

Comprehension Questions

a. 부모님은 아이를 가지기 위해 무엇을 했습니까?

What did the parents do in order to have children?

b. 어떻게 반쪽 아들이 앞마당에 우물을 팠습니까?

How did the half son dig the well in the front yard?

c. 여자의 부모님에게 어떤 일이 일어났습니까? 왜 그들은 반쪽 아들을 멈추지 못했습니까?

What happened to the girl's parents? Why couldn't they stop the half son?

d. 이야기의 마지막에서 반쪽 아들에게 어떤 일이 일어났습니까?

What happened to the half son at the end of the story?

Writing Activity

반쪽 아들이 그 여자를 납치한 행동에 대해 어떻게 생각합니까? 그것이 적절하다고생각합니까? 당신의 의견을 제시하고 이유를 설명하세요.

What do you think about the behavior of the half son when he kidnapped the girl? Do you think it is proper or not? Explain your reasoning.

이야기 귀신

Iyagi Gwisin

옛날 옛날에 이야기를 아주 좋아하는 아이가 살았습니다. 하지만 이야기를 듣는 것만 좋아하고, 남에게 들려 주는 것은 좋아하지 않았습니다. 그 아이는 이야기를 들으면 적어서 이야기 주머니 속에 넣어 두었습니다. 그 아이가 자라서 총각이 되었습니다. 주머니 속에서 오래 산 이야기들은 귀신이 되었습니다. 총각이 결혼하기 전날, 친구와 놀다가 같이 잠들었습니다. 친구는 자다 깨서 이야기 주머니 속의 귀신들이 하는 말을 들었습니다.

"내일 이 놈이 결혼하기 전에 가서 없애 버리자." 한 귀신이 말했습니다. "나는 결혼하는 길에 열린 배가 되어서, 이놈이 먹으면 죽게 할 거야." 다른 귀신이 말했습니다. "나는 신부 옆의 바늘 방석이 되어서, 이놈이 앉으면 죽게 할 거야." 또 다른 귀신이 말했습니다.

친구는 아주 걱정이 되어서 다음날 결혼하러 가는 길에 따라갔습니다. 총각은 배가 고파서 배를 먹고 싶어했습니다. 하지만, 친구는 먹지 못하게 하고 빨리 걸었습니다. 신부의 집에 도착했을 때, 총각은 신부의 옆 방석에 앉고 싶었습니다. 하지만 친구가 바늘방석을 보고 총각을 밀어서 넘어졌습니다. 총각은 아주 부끄러웠습니다. 그래서 친구에게 화를 냈습니다. 친구는 전날 밤에 들었던 귀신들의 이야기를 말해 주었습니다. 총각은 친구에게 사과하고 이야기 주머니를 열어서 귀신들을 풀어 주었습니다.

❖ ❖ ❖

66

The Story Ghost

❖ *This story is about ghosts who fail to disrupt a happy wedding day.* ❖

Once upon a time, there was a boy who loved stories. He only loved listening to stories, but did not love to tell the stories to others. When the boy listened to a story, he would write down the story and put it in his story pocket. The boy became a man. The stories lived in that pocket for a long time and eventually became ghosts. A day before the man got married, he and his friend fell asleep while entertaining themselves. The friend later awoke from his sleep and listened to the conversation of the ghosts in the pocket.

"Let's kill him before he gets married," a ghost said. "I am going to be a hanging pear on the road to the wedding and if he eats it, I will make him die."

Another ghost said, "I am going to be a needle in a cushion that is next to the bride, and if he sits on it I will make him die."

The friend, now worried about the man, followed the man on his way to marriage the next day. The man was hungry and wanted to eat a pear he saw. However, the friend interrupted him and walked him quickly past the pear. When they arrived at the bride's house, the man wanted to sit on the cushion that was next to the bride. However, the friend saw a needle in the cushion and pushed the man causing him to fall down. The man became very embarrassed and got angry at his friend. Then his friend told him the story of the ghosts that he heard the night before. The man said he was sorry to the friend and opened the story pocket and released the ghosts.

❖ ❖ ❖

Pre-Reading Questions (answer in Korean or English)

a. 어떤 사건이 설명되거나 묘사될 것이라고 생각합니까?

  What event do you think is being explained or described?

b. 이것은 실제 이야기처럼 보입니까? 아니면 가상의 이야기처럼 보입니까? 왜 그렇게 생각합니까?

  Does this seem like a real or imaginary story? Why?

c. 당신이 들었던 가장 무서운 이야기는 무엇이었습니까?

  What is the scariest story you have heard?

Vocabulary

이야기 **iyagi** a story

아이 **ai** a child (boy or girl)

하지만 **hajiman** but/however

듣다 **deudda** to listen

~만 **man** only ~

남 **nam** others

들려 주다 **deullyeo juda** to tell

적다 **jeogda** to write

주머니 **jumeoni** a pocket

넣어 두다 **neoh-eo duda** to put something in

자라다 **jalada** to grow up

총각 **chong-gag** a bachelor

오래 **olae** for a long time

귀신 **gwisin** a ghost

되다 **doeda** to become

전날 **jeonnal** a day before

놀다 **nolda** to play

잠들다 **jamdeulda** to fall asleep

깨다 **kkaeda** to awake

배 **bae** a pear

다른 **daleun** different

바늘 **baneul** a needle

방석 **bangseog** a cushion

걱정 **geugjeong** a concern

따라가다 **ddalagada** to follow

밀다 **milda** to push

넘어지다 **neom-eojida** to fall down

Culture Notes

In the old days, Korean people believed there were spirits in old objects. Therefore, an object that was passed on from grandmother to mother, and then to their daughter was cherished. Even when the objects became broken, they prayed or held memorial ceremonies before throwing them away.

Comprehension Questions

a. 어떤 사건들이 일어났습니까? 그 사건들은 어떤 순서로 일어납니까?

What are the specific incidents or events that occur? In what order do they happen?

b. 어떤 것이 이 이야기에서 가장 중요한 사건을 일어나게 했습니까?

What caused the major event in this story?

Writing Activity

명함 크기의 종이에 가장 흥미진진한 방식으로 이 이야기를 다시 써 보십시오. 반친구들과 그 이야기를 같이 읽으십시오. 왜 그것들을 당신의 이야기에 넣었습니까? 당신의 이야기는 다른 친구들의 이야기와 같습니까?

On paper the size of a business card, rewrite the story in the most exciting way you can. Share it with the class. Why did you include what you did? Does your story match other students' stories?

우렁이 신부

Uleong-i Sinbu

옛날 옛날에 결혼을 하지 못한 노총각이 살았습니다. 노총각은 너무 외로웠습니다. 그래서 일을 하며 혼자 말했습니다. "이렇게 일해서 누구랑 같이 먹고 사나?"

그랬더니 누군가가 대답했습니다. "나랑 같이 먹고 살지."

노총각은 깜짝 놀랐습니다. 그래서 다시 한 번 말했습니다. "이렇게 일해서 누구랑 같이 먹고 사나?"

그랬더니 누군가가 또 대답했습니다. "나랑 같이 먹고 살지."

노총각은 다시 깜짝 놀랐습니다. 소리가 난 곳을 보니 우렁이가 있었습니다. 노총각은 우렁이를 집에 데려 왔습니다. 다음 날, 노총각이 일을 하고 나서 점심을 먹으려고 집에 오자 밥이 차려져 있었습니다. 누가 했는지 궁금했지만 배가 고파서 그냥 밥을 먹었습니다. 그 다음 날에도 노총각이 집에 오자 밥이 차려져 있었습니다. 노총각은 누가 밥을 차렸는지 아주 궁금했습니다. 그래서 일하러 가는 척 하고 부엌에 숨었습니다.

그러자 우렁이가 아주 예쁜 여자로 변해서 밥을 차렸습니다. 노총각은 여자에게 가서 결혼하자고 말했습니다. 노총각과 우렁이 신부는 행복하게 살았습니다.

❖ ❖ ❖

The Freshwater Snail Bride

❖ This story is about a man and his beautiful wife. ❖

Once upon a time, there was an old bachelor. The old bachelor was very lonely. One day he said to himself while working, "If I work like this, who can I live with?"

Then, someone answered, "You are going to live with me."

The old bachelor was so surprised, he repeated himself one more time, "If I work like this, who can I live with?"

Then, someone answered again, "You are going to live with me."

The old bachelor was again surprised. When he looked to the place from whence the answer came, there was a freshwater snail. The old bachelor brought the freshwater snail home with him. The next day, when the old bachelor came home for lunch after working, his lunch was already prepared. He wondered who did it, but just ate because he was so hungry. On the following day, when the old bachelor came home, the lunch was already prepared again. The old bachelor really began to wonder who prepared the lunch. Then, the old bachelor pretended he was going to work and hid himself in the kitchen.

The freshwater snail changed into a very beautiful woman and prepared the lunch. The old bachelor went to the woman and asked her to marry him. The old bachelor and the freshwater snail bride lived happily ever after.

❖ ❖ ❖

71

Pre-Reading Questions (answer in Korean or English)

a. 어떤 사건이 설명되거나 묘사될 것이라고 생각합니까?

   What event do you think is being explained or described?

b. 제목에 대해 어떻게 생각합니까?

   What are your feelings about the title?

c. 이 이야기가 대답했으면 하는 질문은 무엇입니까?

   What questions do you hope this story will answer?

Vocabulary

하지 못하다 **haji motada** cannot do something

노총각 **nochong-gag** an old bachelor

외롭다 **oelobda** to be lonely

일 **il** to work/a work

혼자 **honja** alone

누구/누군가 **nugu/nugun-ga** someone

같이 **gachi** together

먹고 살다 **meoggo salda** to live (lit., eat and live)

대답하다 **daedapada** to answer

소리 **soli** a sound

우렁이 **uleong-i** a freshwater snail

점심 **jeomsim** lunch

차려져 있다 **chalyeojyeo idda** to be prepared (food)

궁금하다 **gung-geumhada** to be curious

배가 고프다 **baega gopeuda** to be hungry

그냥 **geunyang** just because

~척 하다 **cheog hada** to pretend ~

부엌 **bu-eok** a kitchen

숨다 **sumda** to hide

예쁘다 **yeppeuda** to be pretty

변하다 **byeonhada** to be changed

다시 **dasi** again

또 **ddo** also, again

일하러 가다 **ilhaleo gada** to go to work

그러자 **geureoja** then/and then

여자 **yeoja** a woman

행복하게 살다 **haengboghage salda** to live happily

Culture Notes

In Korea, people call an old man who has not been married **No-chong-gak. No** means "being old" and **chong-gak** means a man who is not married. **No-cheo-nyeo**, on the other hand, refers to a woman who has not been married. These two titles are fairly derogatory. Unless you want to offend someone, you should not call people by these names.

Comprehension Questions

a. 어떤 사건들이 일어났습니까? 그 사건들은 어떤 순서로 일어납니까?

   What are the specific incidents or events that occur? In what order do they happen?

b. 어떤 것이 이 이야기에서 가장 중요한 사건을 일어나게 했습니까?

   What caused the major event in this story?

Writing Activity

이 이야기 속 등장인물들의 성별을 바꾸고, 성별이 다른 경우 등장인물들의 성격이 어떻게 달라질지를 보여 주기 위해 이야기의 부분들을 다시 쓰십시오.

Change the characters' genders in this story and rewrite the story to show how the characters might act differently.

선녀와 나무꾼

Seonnyeowa Namukkun

옛날 옛날에 나무꾼이 숲 속에서 나무를 하고 있었습니다. 그때, 사슴이 나무꾼에게 뛰어 와서 말했습니다. "나무꾼님, 나 좀 숨겨 주세요. 사냥꾼이 쫓아와요." 나무꾼이 사슴을 숨겨 주었습니다.

조금 있다가 사냥꾼이 나무꾼에게 뛰어와서 물었습니다. "사슴 한 마리 못 봤습니까?"

나무꾼은 모르는 척 하고 대답했습니다. "저 쪽으로 갔습니다." 사냥꾼은 나무꾼의 거짓말을 믿고 그 쪽으로 갔습니다.

숨어 있던 사슴이 나와서 나무꾼에게 고맙다고 했습니다. "고맙습니다, 나무꾼님. 혹시 결혼하고 싶으면 보름달이 뜨는 날 밤에 연못으로 가세요. 그러면 선녀들이 목욕을 하러 내려옵니다. 제일 예쁜 선녀의 날개옷을 감추면 그 선녀와 결혼할 수 있어요."

나무꾼은 보름달이 뜨는 날 밤에 연못에 가서 숨어 있었습니다. 선녀 세 명이 하늘에서 내려와서 목욕을 했습니다. 나무꾼은 제일 예쁜 셋째 선녀의 날개옷을 감췄습니다. 목욕을 다 하고, 첫째와 둘째 선녀는 날개옷을 입고 하늘로 다시 돌아갔습니다. 하지만 셋째 선녀는 하늘로 돌아가지 못해서 나무꾼과 결혼할 수밖에 없었습니다. 나무꾼과 셋째 선 녀는 행복하게 살면서 아이를 세 명 낳았습니다. 어느 날, 나무꾼은 셋째 선녀에게 아주 미안해하면서 날개옷을 돌려주었습니다. 그리고 다음 날, 나무꾼이 나무를 하러 갔을 때 아이들이 "아버지, 아버지!" 하고 불렀습니다. 하늘을 보자 셋째 선녀가 날개옷을 입고 아이 둘을 양팔에 안고 한명은 등에 업고 하늘로 올라가고 있었습니다. 나무꾼은 엉엉 울었습니다.

❖ ❖ ❖

The Fairy and the Woodcutter

✤ *This story is about a woodcutter who married a fairy.* ✤

Once upon a time, a woodcutter was cutting some wood in a forest. At that time, a deer ran to the woodcutter and said, "Mr. Woodcutter, please hide me. A hunter is chasing me." The woodcutter hid the deer.

After a little while, the hunter ran up to the woodcutter and asked, "Did you see a deer?"

The woodcutter pretended that he didn't know anything and answered, "It went that way." The hunter believed the woodcutter's lie and went the way he suggested.

The deer who had been hiding came out to thank the woodcutter: "Thank you, Mr. Woodcutter. If you want to marry, go to the pond at night when there is a full moon and fairies will come down for a bath. If you hide the robe of feathers from the most beautiful fairy, you can marry her."

The woodcutter went to the pond at night when the full moon was full and hid himself. Three fairies came down from the sky and took a bath. The woodcutter hid the robe of feathers from the third and most beautiful fairy. After finishing the bath, the first and second fairies put on their robes of feathers and went back to the sky. However, the third fairy could not go back to the sky, and so had no choice but to marry the woodcutter. The woodcutter and the third fairy lived happily and had three children. One day, the woodcutter felt very sorry for the third fairy, so he returned the robe of feathers to her. The next day, when the woodcutter went to cut the wood, his children called after him, "Father, father!" Looking to the sky, the woodcutter saw the third fairy going up toward the sky, wearing the robe of feathers, and holding two children in her arms, and carrying one child on her back. The woodcutter cried loudly.

✤ ✤ ✤

Pre-Reading Questions (answer in Korean or English)

a. 어떤 사건이 설명되거나 묘사될 것이라고 생각합니까?

   What event do you think is being explained or described?

b. 제목이 주는 이 이야기에 대한 단서는 무엇입니까?

   What clues does the title give you about the story?

c. 이 이야기에서 중요한 등장인물을 추측할 수 있습니까?

   Can you guess the major figures or characters that play a part in this story?

Vocabulary

나무꾼 **namu-kkun** a woodcutter

그때 **geu-ttae** at that time

사슴 **saseum** a deer

뛰어오다 **ttwi-eo-oda** to run (to someone)

숨겨 주다 **sumgyeo juda** to hide (someone)

사냥꾼 **sa-nyang-kkun** a hunter

쫓아오다 **jjoch-aoda** to chase

보다 **boda** to see

못 **mos** can't do

모르는 척 하다 **mo-leu-neun cheog hada** to pretend you don't

저 쪽 **jeo jjog** that way

거짓말 **geojismal** a lie

믿다 **midda** to believe

고맙다고 하다 **gomabdago hada** to say thank you

보름달 **boleumdal** a full moon

뜨다 **tteuda** to rise (the moon or sun)

연못 **yeonmos** a pond

선녀 **seonnyeo** a fairy (Taoist fairy)

목욕 **mog-yog** a bath

제일 **jeil** the most

예쁘다 **yeppeuda** to be beautiful

날개옷 **nalgaeos** a robe of feathers

다시 **dasi** again

돌아가다 **dol-agada** to go back

낳다 **nahda** to give birth

부르다 **bu-leuda** to call

업다 **eobda** to carry (someone) on your back

Culture Notes

Seon-nyeo are like fairies who live with God in heaven. They are usually female, and they wear clothes that have wings so they can fly. They are usually described as very beautiful women. Therefore, in the old days people called a beautiful woman "a woman like **Seon-nyeo**."

Comprehension Questions

a. 이 이야기에서 한 등장인물이 다른 선택을 했다면 이야기가 어떻게 달라질 지를 반친구들이나 옆사람과 토론하십시오.

Discuss as a class or with a partner how the story might have changed if one character had made a different choice.

b. 이 이야기에 나오는 한 등장인물의 독백을 만드십시오. 그들은 주어진 순간 마다 어떤 생각을 하고 무엇을 느낍니까? 왜 그렇습니까?

Create a monologue for a character in the story. What are they thinking or feeling in each given moment? Why?

Writing Activity

책에 나오는 다른 등장인물의 관점에서 이야기를 다시 쓰십시오.

Rewrite the story from the point of view of a different character in the book.

여우와 할머니

Yeouwa Halmeoni

옛날 옛날에 형제가 살았습니다. 형은 욕심이 많고 동생은 착했습니다. 어느 날 부모님이 돌아가셨는데, 형이 돈을 다 가져가고 동생에게는 아무 것도 주지 않았습니다. 그래서 동생은 여기저기 돌아다니며 소금 장사를 하기 시작했습니다. 그러던 어느 날, 동생이 아직 산 속에 있는데 밤이 되어서 어떤 무덤 근처에서 잠을 자게 되었습니다. 동생은 이상한 소리가 나서 잠에서 깨었습니다. 소리 나는 쪽으로 가서 보자 여우 한 마리가 무덤을 파서 해골을 머리에 써 보고 있었습니다. 머리에 딱 맞는 해골을 쓰고 세 번 재주를 넘더니 할머니로 변했습니다. 동생은 조심해서 여우를 따라갔습니다. 여우는 어떤 집에 도착했고, 사람들은 여우가 할머니인 줄 알았습니다. 여우는 사람들을 잡아먹고 싶어했습니다. 하지만 동생이 달려가서 막대기로 여우를 때렸습니다. 사람들은 놀라서 화를 내려고 했지만, 할머니가 여우로 변해서 죽는 것을 보고 동생에게 고마워하며 돈을 주었습니다.

욕심 많은 형도 동생처럼 돈을 받고 싶었습니다. 그래서 지나가는 할머니를 막대기로 때렸습니다. 하지만 그 할머니는 여우가 아니었습니다. 할머니의 가족들이 화가 나서 형을 때렸습니다. 착한 동생은 형을 데리고 자신의 집에 가서 잘 보살펴 주었습니다.

❖ ❖ ❖

The Fox and the Old Woman

❖ *This story is about a suspicious fox and two brothers.* ❖

Once upon a time, there were two brothers. The older brother was greedy and the younger brother was kind. One day, their parents died, and the older brother took all of the money, giving nothing to the younger brother. Therefore, the younger brother started to sell salt, wandering from here to there. Then one day, the younger brother had to sleep next to a graveyard, as night had come and he was still in the mountains. The younger brother was awakened from his sleep by strange sounds. When he went over to where the sounds were coming from, he saw a fox digging a grave and trying to wear a skull on its head. The fox wore the skull that fit on its head, did three cartwheels, and became an old woman. The younger brother carefully followed the fox. The fox arrived at a house where the people thought the fox was really an old woman. The fox wanted to eat the people. However, the younger brother ran up to the fox and hit it with a stick. The people became very angry, but when they saw the old woman turn back into the fox and die, the people thankfully gave money to the younger brother.

The greedy older brother saw this and wanted to get a lot of money like his younger brother, so he hit an old woman passing by with a stick. However, the old woman was not a fox. The family of the old woman attacked the older brother because they were so angry. The kind younger brother brought the older brother to his house and took good care of him.

❖ ❖ ❖

79

Pre-Reading Questions (answer in Korean or English)

a. 여우가 전래동화에서 가지는 공통적 성격은 무엇입니까? 여우가 이 이야기에서도 똑같은 성격을 가질 거라고 생각합니까? 왜 그렇습니까?

What are some common characteristics that foxes have in folktales? Do you think those characteristics will be true of the fox in this story? Why or why not?

b. 이 이야기에서 여우와 할머니의 관계를 추측할 수 있습니까?

Can you guess the relationship between the fox and the old woman in this story?

Vocabulary

형제 **hyeongje** the brothers

욕심 **yogsim** greed

많다 **manhda** to be a lot

착하다 **chaghada** to be kind

부모님 **bumonim** the parents

돌아가시다 **dol-agasida** to die (*honorific*)

다 **da** all of ~

가져가다 **gajyeogada** to take, to bring

아무것도 주지 않다 **amugeosdo juji anhda** to give nothing

그래서 **geu-laeseo** therefore

여기저기 **yeogijeogi** from here to there

돌아다니다 **dol-adanida** to wander

소금 **sogeum** salt

장사 **jangsa** a sale

무덤 **mudeom** a grave

깨다 **kkaeda** to be awakened from

여우 **yeou** a fox

해골 **haegol** a skull

머리 **meoli** a head

쓰다 **sseuda** to wear

재주를 넘다 **jaejuleul neomda** to do cartwheels

할머니 **halmeoni** an old woman

도착하다 **dochaghada** to arrive

막대기 **magdaegi** a stick

지나가다 **jinagada** to pass by

때리다 **ttae-lida** to hit

보살펴 주다 **bosalpyeo juda** to take care of someone

Culture Notes

In old Korean stories, foxes can often transform into something else. The most famous of such foxes is Gu-mi-ho, a fox with nine tails. They say a fox that has lived for a thousand years turns into Gu-mi-ho. It never dies, and often transforms to a beautiful woman so it can lure people close enough to be its prey. It likes to eat human liver, and it is said that when it eats a thousand human livers it can become a human.

Comprehension Questions

a. 이 이야기에 나오는 형제의 성격은 어떻습니까?

What were some of the characteristics of the two brothers in this story?

b. 여우는 어떻게 할머니로 바뀌었습니까?

How did the fox change into the old woman?

c. 왜 형은 할머니를 때렸습니까?

Why did the older brother hit the old woman?

Writing Activity

이 이야기에서 한 등장인물이 다른 선택을 했다면 이야기가 어떻게 달라질지를 반친구들이나 옆사람과 토론하십시오.

Discuss as a class or with a partner how the story might have changed if one character had made a different choice in the story.

거지 형제

Geoji Hyeongje

옛날 옛날에 한 형제가 살았습니다. 부모님은 형제가 어렸을 때 돌아가셔서, 형과 동생은 여기저기 돌아다니면서 음식을 얻어 먹었습니다. 형이 아주 욕심이 많아서 동생이 자기보다 더 많이 얻어 먹으면 화를 내었습니다. 어느 날 형이 말했습니다. "나는 큰 집만 있는 동네에 가서 음식을 얻어 먹을 테니까, 너는 작은 집만 있는 동네에 가서 음식을 얻어 먹어라." 착한 동생은 그대로 했습니다. 그런데, 그 날 큰 집만 있는 동네는 다들 아파서 형에게 문을 열어 주지 않았습니다. 작은 집만 있는 동네는 집집마다 잔치를 해서 동생은 많은 음식을 먹었습니다. 동생이 음식을 많이 가져오자 형은 화가 났습니다. 그래서 다시 말했습니다. "내일은 내가 작은 집만 있는 동네에 갈 테니까, 너는 내일 큰 집만 있는 동네에 가라." 동생은 또 그대로 했습니다. 그런데 작은 집만 있는 동네는 잔치가 끝나서 먹을 것이 없었습니다. 큰 집만 있는 동네는 아프지 않으려고 음식을 많이 해서 동생은 또 많은 음식을 먹었습니다.

❖ ❖ ❖

The Beggar Brothers

❖   *This story is about two brothers and their different behaviors.*   ❖

Once upon a time, there were two brothers. Their parents passed away when they were young, so the older brother and the younger brother begged for food while wandering here and there. The older brother always got angry if the younger brother got more food than he did, because he was very greedy. One day, the older brother said, "I will beg for food at a village that only has big houses, so you go to a village that only has small houses and beg for food." The nice younger brother did as he was told. However, on that particular day, the village that only had big houses did not open their doors for the older brother because they were all sick. The village that only had small houses had a party at every house, so the younger brother ate a lot of food. When the younger brother brought a lot of food back, the older brother became angry. This time he said, "I will go to the village that only has small houses tomorrow. You go to the village that only has big houses tomorrow." The younger brother once again did as he was asked. However, there was nothing to eat at the village that only had small houses because the parties were over. The village that only had big houses made a lot of food because they did not want to stay sick, so the younger brother once again ate a lot of food.

❖ ❖ ❖

Pre-Reading Questions (answer in Korean or English)

a. 어떤 사건이 설명되거나 묘사될 것이라고 생각합니까?

   What event do you think is being explained or described?

b. 제목이 주는 이 이야기에 대한 단서는 무엇입니까?

   What clues does the title give you about the story?

c. 이 이야기에서 중요한 등장인물을 추측할 수 있습니까?

   Can you guess the major figures or characters that play a part in this story?

Vocabulary

어렸을 때 **eolyeoss-eul ttae** when you were young

여기저기 **yeogijeogi** from here to there

돌아다니다 **dol-adanida** to wander

얻어먹다 **eod-eomeogda** to beg for food (and eat)

아주 **aju** very

욕심이 많다 **yogsim-i manhda** to be greedy

욕심이 많아서 **yogsim-i manh-aseo** because you are greedy

자기보다 더 많이 **jagiboda deo manh-i** more than oneself

화를 내다 **hwaleul naeda** to get angry

큰 집 **keun jib** a big house

작은 집 **jag-eun jib** a small house

동네 **dongne** a village

~만 있는 … **~man issneun …** … that only has ~

착한 ~ **chaghan ~** a nice ~ (person)

그대로 하다 **geudaelo hada** to do as someone is told

그런데 **geuleonde** however

그 날 **geu nal** on that particular day

다들 **dadeul** everyone

아프다 **apeuda** to be sick

아파서 **apaseo** because you are sick

문 **mun** a door

열다 **yeolda** to open

집집마다 **jibjibmada** at every house

잔치 **janchi** a (traditional) party

다시 / 또 **dasi / tto** again

끝나서 **kkeutnaseo** because it is ended/over

아프지 않으려고 **apeuji anh-eulyeo-go** to avoid getting sick

Culture Notes

In this story, the younger brother visits a village that is throwing a party. In Korea, this is called a **Jan-chi** party, where a house owner invites guests over for a meal. Usually, they throw a **Jan-chi** when they want to welcome or say farewell to someone. In the old days, people did not get to eat meat very often because it was too expensive. Cows and pigs were rarely butchered for food. However, on a party day they prepared meat for their guests, and everyone enjoyed eating, singing, and dancing.

Comprehension Questions

a. 이 이야기에 나오는 형제의 성격은 어떻습니까?

    What are the characteristics of two brothers in this story?

b. 형이 처음에 음식을 많이 먹을 수 없었던 이유는 무엇입니까?

    What is the reason that the older brother could not get a lot of food the first time?

c. 어떻게 동생이 항상 음식을 많이 먹을 수 있었습니까?

    How was the younger brother always able to get a lot of food?

Writing Activity

이 이야기의 결과에 따라 당신의 믿음이 더 강해졌는지 혹은 이의를 가지게 되었는지 토론하십시오. 이 이야기가 주는 교훈에 동의하십니까?

Discuss how your beliefs were either strengthened or challenged as a result of the themes in this story. Do you agree or disagree with the lessons presented?

화수분 바가지

Hwasubun Bagaji

옛날 옛날에 가난한 농사꾼이 살았습니다. 가난하지만 아주 착한 사람이었습니다. 어느 날, 농사가 잘 되지 않아서 먹을 것이 없었습니다. 농사꾼은 먹을 것을 사러 밖에 나갔습니다. 어떤 사람이 개구리를 잔뜩 잡아서 가고 있었습니다. 농사꾼이 물었습니다. "개구리는 어디에 쓰려고 잡아 가세요?" 그 사람이 대답했습니다. "집에 먹을 것이 없어서 개구리라도 먹으려고 해요." 농사꾼은 개구리들이 불쌍하다고 생각했습니다. 그래서 그 사람에게 돈을 주고 개구리를 전부 사서, 연못에 넣어 주었습니다. 개구리들이 '개굴개굴' 하면서 농사꾼에게 바가지 하나를 주었습니다. 농사꾼은 그 바가지를 들고 집에 왔습니다. 집에 먹을 것은 쌀 한 컵 밖에 없었습니다. 하지만 신기하게도 그 쌀을 바가지에 넣자 쌀이 계속 계속 생겨났습니다. 개구리들이 은혜를 갚은 것입니다. 착한 농사꾼은 이 쌀을 이웃 사람들에게 나누어 주었습니다. 이렇게 무엇이 계속 계속 생겨나는 것을 화수분이라고 합니다.

❖ ❖ ❖

The *Hwasubun* Bowl

❖   *This story is about a bowl that has mysterious power.*   ❖

Once upon a time, there was a poor farmer. Although he was poor, he was a very nice person. One day, there was nothing to eat because farming was not going well for him. The farmer went outside to buy something to eat. A person was going somewhere with a lot of frogs he had caught.

The farmer asked, "Where are you going to use those frogs?"

The person answered, "Because there is nothing to eat at my house, I am going to eat the frogs."

The farmer felt very bad for the frogs. So, he gave money to the man and bought all of the frogs, and put them into a pond. The frogs gave a bowl to the farmer while croaking "ribbit, ribbit." The farmer brought the bowl with him and went back to his house. There was only a cup of rice to eat at his house. However, when he put the rice into the bowl, the rice continued to grow and grow, by magic. It was the frogs repaying his kindness. The kind farmer passed around the rice to his neighbors. As seen in this story, "Hwasubun" means that something is becoming and growing into more and more.

❖ ❖ ❖

Pre-Reading Questions (answer in Korean or English)

a. 제목에 이 이야기에 대한 단서가 있습니까?

   Is there any clue about this story from the title?

b. 이야기가 일어나는 배경을 추측할 수 있습니까?

   Can you guess the setting where the story might occur?

c. "화수분"에 대해서 들어 본 적이 있습니까?

   Have you ever heard about the "Hwasubun" before?

Vocabulary

가난하다 **gananhada** to be poor

농사꾼 **nongsakkun** a farmer

가난하지만 **gananhajiman** although you are poor

아주 **aju** very

농사 **nongsa** farming

잘 되지 않다 **jal doeji anhda** to not be working well

먹을 것 **meog-eul geos** something to eat

없다 **eobsda** there is nothing/no one

사다 **sada** to buy

밖에 나가다 **bakk-e nagada** to go outside

어떤 사람 **eotteon salam** a person, someone

잔뜩 **jantteug** a lot of

잡다 **jabda** to catch

묻다 **mudda** to ask

어디에 쓰려고 **eodie sseulyeogo** to use it for what

불쌍하다 **bulssanghada** to be poor, pathetic

돈 **don** money

전부 **jeonbu** all

넣어 주다 **neoh-eo juda** to put

개굴개굴 **gaegulgaegul** ribbit ribbit

바가지 **bagaji** a bowl

한 컵 **han keob** a (one) cupful

넣다 **neohda** to put it into somewhere

계속 **gyesog** a (traditional) party

생겨나다 **saeng-gyeonada** to continue to grow

은혜를 갚다 **eunhyeleul gapda** to repay one's kindness

나누어 주다 **nanueo juda** to pass around, share

Culture Notes

In this story, the protagonist saved the life of a frog, and as a result received a **Hawsubun** (magical pot that provides money and rice). Likewise, in the old days people believed that good things happened when they helped animals in danger. They also believed that animals have spirits, and animals who lived long lives have mysterious powers.

Comprehension Questions

a. 왜 가난한 농사꾼은 개구리를 도와 주었습니까?

   Why did the poor farmer help the frogs?

b. 개구리는 가난한 농사꾼에게 무엇을 주었습니까?

   What did the frogs give the poor farmer?

c. 그것은 가난한 농사꾼을 위해 어떤 일을 했습니까?

   How did it work for the poor farmer?

Writing Activity

명함 크기의 종이에 가장 흥미진진한 방식으로 이 이야기를 다시 써 보십시오. 반친구들과 그 이야기를 같이 읽으십시오. 왜 그것들을 당신의 이야기에 넣었습니까?당신의 이야기는 다른 친구들의 이야기와 같습니까?

Rewrite the story in the most exciting way you can on paper the size of a business card (in Korean or in English) Share it with the class. Why did you include what you did? Does your story match other students' stories?

호랑이 잡는 망태기

Holang-i Jabneun Mangtaegi

옛날 옛날에 가난한 총각이 살았습니다. 너무 너무 가난해서 먹을 것을 찾으러 산으로 갔는데 그만 밤이 되고 말았습니다. 여기 저기 돌아다니다가 한 집을 발견했고, 집 주인 할아버지에게 하룻밤만 자고 가겠다고 말했습니다. 할아버지는 총각에게 들어오라고 말했습니다. 할아버지는 짚으로 망태기를 만들고 있었습니다. 총각이 물었습니다.

"왜 망태기를 만들고 계세요?"

할아버지가 대답했습니다.

"가난한 사람이 여기에 들어가면 돈이 많아지지."

총각은 귀가 솔깃해졌습니다. 총각이 물었습니다.

"그럼 제가 들어가도 될까요?"

할아버지가 대답했습니다. "그래도 되지."

총각은 다 만들어진 망태기에 들어갔습니다. 그러자, 할아버지가 갑자기 망태기 입구를 꽉 묶어서 산 속 큰 나뭇가지에 걸어 놓았습니다. 총각은 무서워서 소리를 질렀습니다. 하지만 할아버지는 나무 밑에 뾰족한 말뚝을 여러 개 박아 놓고 다시 집으로 가 버렸습니다.

밤이 깊었습니다. 호랑이들이 나무에 매달린 총각을 먹으려고 다가왔습니다. 하지만 총각을 먹으려고 펄쩍 펄쩍 뛰다가 나무 밑의 말뚝에 찔려 죽었습니다. 다음 날 아침, 할아버지는 총각에게 나무 밑에 죽어 있는 호랑이들을 주었습니다. 총각은 호랑이들을 팔아서 부자가 되었습니다.

❖ ❖ ❖

The Net Bag for Catching a Tiger

✤   *This story is about how a man became rich.*   ✤

Once upon a time, there was a poor young bachelor. Because he was really poor, he went to the mountains to find something to eat, but then it became nighttime. He found a house while wandering around and asked the old man who was the owner of the house, if he could sleep there for one night. The old man told the bachelor to come in. The old man was making a net bag with straw.

The bachelor asked, "Why are you making a net bag?"

The old man answered, "If a poor person goes into this net, that person will get a lot of money."

The bachelor was very interested, and asked, "May I get into the bag?"

The old man answered, "Of course."

He got into the net bag, which had just been finished. Then, the old man suddenly tied up the mouth of the net bag tightly and hung it on a big branch on the mountain. The man screamed because he was scared. The old man embedded several sharp stakes under the tree and went back to his house. It grew late. Tigers came closer and closer to eat the man hanging in the tree. However, as they jumped up to eat him, they were impaled on the stakes under the tree. The next morning, the old man gave the dead tigers under the tree to the bachelor. He then sold the tigers and became rich.

✤   ✤   ✤

Pre-Reading Questions (answer in Korean or English)

a. 어떤 사건이 설명되거나 묘사될 것이라고 생각합니까?

b. 이 이야기에서 중요한 물건이나 등장인물을 추측할 수 있습니까?

c. 제목과 부제목이 주는 이 이야기에 대한 단서는 무엇입니까?

Vocabulary

망태기 **mangtaegi** a net bag

가난하다 **gananhada** to be poor

총각 **chong-gag** a bachelor

찾다 **chajda** to find

산으로 **san-eulo** to the mountain

밤 **bam** the night

~이 되고 말다 **~i doego malda** to become … (negative)

발견하다 **balgyeonhada** to discover/ to find

할아버지 **hal-abeoji** an old man/ grandfather

하룻밤 **halusbam** one night

하룻밤만 **halusbamman** only one night

자다 **jada** to sleep

자고 가다 **jago gada** to sleep over

들어오다 **deul-eooda** to come in

짚 **jip** a straw

만들다 **mandeulda** to make

만들고 있다 **mandeulgo issda** to be making

왜 **wae** why

여기 **yeogi** here

많아지다 **manh-ajida** to pile up

귀가 솔깃해지다 **gwiga solgishaejida** to be very interested

~어/아도 될까요? **~eo/ado doelkkayo?** May I ~?

입구 **ibgu** an entrance/mouth of

꽉 묶다 **kkwag mukkda** to tie up tightly

나뭇가지 **namusgaji** a branch

소리를 지르다 **solileul jileuda** to scream

뾰족하다 **ppyojoghada** to be sharp, pointy

Culture Notes

A **mang-tae** is a bag made out of dry straw and shouldered with ropes. Old men (**hal-ah-beo-ji**) used to carry such bags around. It was believed that some of these men were ghosts who would kidnap children who lied or did bad things, by stuffing them into their bags. Therefore, when a child did something bad, people used to scare him by saying, "**Mang-tae Hal-ah-beo-ji** will take you!"

Comprehension Questions

a. 할아버지가 무엇을 만들고 있었습니까?
b. 할아버지는 어떻게 총각을 도와주었습니까? 왜 그것을 했습니까?
c. 총각은 어떻게 부자가 되었습니까?

Writing Activity

당신이 총각과 같은 상황이라면 어떻게 할 지에 대해서 짧은 이야기를 하나 쓰십시오.

Write a short story about what you would do if you were in the man's situation.

빨간 부채 파란 부채

Ppalgan Buchae Palan Buchae

옛날 옛날에 착한 할아버지와 욕심쟁이 할아버지 두 사람이 살았습니다. 착한 할아버지는 아주 가난했고, 욕심쟁이 할아버지는 아주 부자였습니다. 어느 날, 한 손님이 욕심쟁이 할아버지를 찾아왔습니다.

"하룻밤만 재워 주세요."

욕심쟁이 할아버지는 손님이 밥을 먹는 게 아까워서 문을 열어 주지 않았습니다. 손님은 착한 할아버지의 집에 찾아갔습니다.

"하룻밤만 재워 주세요."

착한 할아버지는 손님에게 새로 밥을 해 주고 깨끗한 방으로 안내했습니다.

다음 날 아침, 손님은 사라지고 빨간 부채와 파란 부채만 있었습니다. 착한 할아버지는 빨간 부채를 부쳐 보았습니다. 그러자 코가 길어졌습니다. 깜짝 놀란 할아버지는 파란 부채를 부쳐 보았습니다. 그러자 코가 다시 짧아졌습니다. 착한 할아버지는 재미있어서 두 부채를 가지고 다녔습니다.

욕심쟁이 할아버지는 착한 할아버지의 새 부채들이 가지고 싶었습니다. 그래서 착한 할아버지에게 자신의 집을 주고 부채들을 샀습니다. 욕심쟁이 할아버지는 빨간 부채를 계속 부쳤습니다. 코가 계속 계속 길어져서 하늘 위의 신령에게까지 닿았습니다. 신령이 화가 나서 코를 나무에 묶었습니다. 욕심쟁이 할아버지는 그것도 모르고 다시 파란 부채를 부쳤습니다. 하지만 코가 나무에 묶여 있어서 욕심쟁이 할아버지는 하늘로 계속 올라갔습니다. 그 때 신령이 화가 풀려서 나무에 묶었던 코를 풀었습니다.

❖ ❖ ❖

The Red Fan and the Blue Fan

❖ *This story is about two fans and two old men.* ❖

Once upon a time, there were two old men: a nice old man, and a greedy old man. The nice old man was really poor, and the greedy old man was very rich.

One day, a guest visited the greedy old man and asked, "Please let me stay for just one night."

The greedy old man did not open the door for the visitor, thinking only of the food the visitor would eat. The visitor then went to the house of the nice old man and asked, "Please let me stay for just one night."

The nice old man made new rice for the visitor and brought the visitor into a clean room. The next morning, the visitor was gone and there was only a red fan and a blue fan. The nice old man tried to wave the red fan. His nose then grew longer. The old man was surprised and tried to wave the blue fan. When doing this his nose became shorter again. The nice old man carried the two fans around with him because it was fun. The greedy old man wanted to have the nice old man's new fans, and so he gave his house to the nice old man in exchange for the fans. The greedy old man kept waving the red fan. His nose kept growing longer and longer until it reached the god in the sky. The god became angry, then tied his nose to a tree. The greedy old man did not know about it and waved the blue fan again. However, because his nose was tied to the tree, the greedy old man kept going up toward the sky. Then, the god's anger melted away, and he untied the man's nose.

❖ ❖ ❖

Pre-Reading Questions (answer in Korean or English)

a. 부채에 대해서 무엇을 알고 있습니까? 한국의 전통적 부채를 써 본 적이 있나요? 부채가 어떻게 생겼는지 알고 있습니까?

b. 할아버지와 부채는 어떤 관련이 있을 거라고 생각합니까?

Vocabulary

빨간 부채 **ppalgan buchae** a red fan

파란 부채 **palan buchae** a blue fan

욕심쟁이 **yogsimjaeng-i** a greedy person

부자 **buja** a rich person

손님 **sonnim** a guest/a visitor

찾아오다 **chaj-aoda** to visit

재워 주다 **jaewo juda** to let someone stay

아깝다 **akkabda** to grudge something

열어 주지 않다 **yeol-eo juji anhda** to do not open

새로 **saelo** newly

깨끗하다 **kkaekkeushada** to be clean

방 **bang** a room

방으로 안내하다 **bang-eulo annae-hada** to show a person to …

다음 날 아침 **da-eum nal achim** the next morning

사라지다 **salajida** to disappear

(부채를) 부치다 **buchida** to wave (a fan)

코 **ko** a nose

길어지다 **gil-eojida** to grow longer

짧아지다 **jjalb-ajida** to become shorter

가지고 다니다 **gajigo danida** to carry with

가지고 싶다 **gajigo sipda** to want to have

계속 **gyesog** to keep (doing something)

하늘 **haneul** the sky

위 **wi** the top/above

신령 **sinlyeong** God/deity

그것도 모르고 **geugeosdo moleu-go** unaware of something

화가 풀리다 **hwaga pullida** the anger is melted away

Culture Notes

A **buchae** is a fan used to cool a person off. In Korea, you could use a person's fan to guess his social status. In the early summer, the king always gave fans to his subjects as presents. Fans which were more compact and had more decorative layers were given to men of higher status.

Comprehension Questions
a. 왜 욕심쟁이 할아버지는 손님에게 문을 열어주지 않았습니까?
b. 착한 할아버지가 빨간 부채를 부쳤을 때 어떤 일이 일어났습니까?
c. 어떻게 욕심쟁이 할아버지는 착한 할아버지로부터 두 부채를 얻었습니까?

Writing Activity
이야기가 끝난 다음 등장인물들에게 어떤 일이 일어날 것 같은지에 대한 짧은 문단을 하나 쓰세요.

Write a brief paragraph about what you think will happen to the characters after the story ends.

소금 맷돌

Sogeum Maettol

옛날 옛날에 가난한 농사꾼이 살았습니다. 어느 날 농사꾼은 쌀을 조금 사서 집으로 가고 있었습니다. 그러다 한 할아버지가 맷돌을 가지고 쓰러져 있는 것을 보았습니다. 농사꾼은 할아버지를 집에 데려와서 따뜻한 밥을 주었습니다. 할아버지가 고마워하며 맷돌을 주었습니다. 하지만 농사꾼의 집에는 맷돌에 넣을 것이 없었습니다. 그래서 농사꾼은 그냥 맷돌을 돌리면서 생각했습니다.

"이 맷돌에서 쌀이 계속 나왔으면 좋겠다."

그러자 맷돌에서 쌀이 계속 나왔습니다. 농사꾼은 깜짝 놀랐습니다.

"이 맷돌에서 떡이 나왔으면 좋겠다." 하자 맷돌에서 떡이 계속 나왔습니다. 착한 농사꾼은 맷돌에서 나오는 것들을 이웃 사람들에게 나누어 주었습니다. 그 소문을 듣고 도둑이 찾아왔습니다. 도둑은 농사꾼의 집에서 맷돌을 훔쳐서 배를 타고 바다로 갔습니다. 그 때는 소금이 아주 비쌌습니다. 그래서 도둑이 말했습니다.

"이 맷돌에서 소금이 계속 나왔으면 좋겠다."

그러자 맷돌에서 소금이 계속 나왔습니다. 도둑은 맷돌을 계속 돌렸습니다. 소금 때문에 무거워져서 배가 가라앉기 시작했습니다. 하지만 도둑은 욕심 때문에 맷돌을 멈추지 않았습니다. 결국 배가 맷돌과 함께 바다에 가라앉았습니다. 그 때부터 바닷물이 아주 짜졌습니다.

❖ ❖ ❖

The Salt Millstone

❖ This story explains the reason why the sea is salty. ❖

Once upon a time, there was a poor farmer. One day, the farmer bought some rice and went to his house. Along the way, the farmer saw an old man who had fallen while carrying a millstone. The farmer brought the old man back to his house and gave him a bowl of warm rice. The old man appreciated this act of kindness and gave him the millstone. However, there was nothing to put into the millstone at the farmer's house. Therefore, the farmer simply spinned the millstone while thinking, "It would be great if rice came out from this millstone non-stop." As he said this, rice began continuously pouring from the millstone. The farmer was very surprised.

Then he said, "It would be great if rice cakes came out from this millstone," and multiple rice cakes came out of the millstone non-stop. The nice farmer passed around these things from his millstone to his neighbors. Upon hearing this news, a thief came to his house. The thief stole the millstone and rode a boat far out into the ocean.

At that time, salt was very expensive, so the thief said, "It would be great if salt came out from this millstone continuously." And at that moment, salt came out from the millstone non-stop. The thief continued spinning the millstone over and over again. The boat began to sink because it became heavy with all the salt. However, the greedy thief did not stop the millstone. Finally, the boat sank into the ocean with the millstone. From that day on, seawater has always been salty.

❖ ❖ ❖

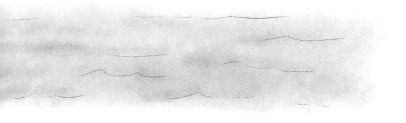

Pre-Reading Questions (answer in Korean or English)

a. 제목이 주는 이 이야기에 대한 단서는 무엇입니까?
b. 이것은 실제 이야기처럼 보입니까? 아니면 가상의 이야기처럼 보입니까? 왜 그렇게 생각합니까?
c. 맷돌에 대해 무엇을 알고 있습니까? 맷돌을 사용해 본 적이 있습니까?

Vocabulary

농사꾼 **nongsakkun** a farmer
조금 **jogeum** a little bit/some
맷돌 **maettol** a millstone
가지다 **gajida** to have
쓰러지다 **sseuleojida** to fall down
쓰러져 있다 **sseuleojyeo issda** to have fallen
데려오다 **delyeooda** to bring (a person)
따뜻하다 **ttatteushada** to be warm
고마워하다 **gomawohada** to appreciate
하지만 **hajiman** but/however
그냥 **geunyang** just/just because
돌리다 **dollida** to spin
생각하다 **saeng-gaghada** to think
그러자 **geuleoja** then/and then

~았/었으면 좋겠다 **~ass/eoss-eu-myeon** it would be great if ~
나오다 **naoda** to come out
이웃 사람들 **ius salamdeul** the neighbors
소문 **somun** some news/a rumor
도둑 **dodug** a thief
훔치다 **humchida** to steal
바다 **bada** the sea
그 때 **geu ttae** at that time
소금 **sogeum** salt
비싸다 **bissada** to be expensive
무거워지다 **mugeowojida** to become heavy
가라앉다 **galaanjda** to sink
짜지다 **jjajida** to be salty

Culture Notes

A **maettol** is a tool that is used to grind soaked beans or to make flour. It comes in various sizes, from 20 cm to 1 m in diameter. Big **meattol** were usually used in temples because the monks made a lot of tofu instead of eating meat.

Comprehension Questions

a. 농부는 어떻게 맷돌을 얻었습니까?
b. 맷돌의 신기한 힘은 무엇이었습니까?
c. 도둑이 한 행동의 결과는 무엇이었습니까?

Writing Activity

이 이야기의 사건들을 순서대로 표시하세요. 화이트보드에 포스트잇을 사용해서 사건의 순서를 표시하십시오. 다른 학생들이 표시한 순서와 일치합니까?

Create a timeline that shows the events in this story. Use Post-it notes on the whiteboard to show the timeline. Does your timeline match the other students' timelines?

은혜 갚은 까치

Eunhye Gap-eun Kkachi

옛날 옛날에 한 총각이 산 너머 마을에 가고 있었습니다. 가는 길에 큰 뱀 한 마리가 까치를 잡아먹으려고 나무에 올라가는 것을 보았습니다. 총각이 까치를 도우려고 뱀을 활로 쏴서 죽였습니다.

그리고 나서, 총각이 아직 산 속에 있는데 밤이 되고 말았습니다. 총각은 산 속에서 집을 하나 찾아서 들어갔습니다. 집 주인은 한 여자였습니다. 총각은 너무 피곤해서 밥을 먹고 바로 잠이 들었습니다. 자다가 숨이 막혀서 일어나 보자 큰 뱀이 총각의 몸을 감고 있었습니다.

"네가 활을 쏴서 죽인 그 뱀이 내 남편이다. 네가 내 남편을 죽였으니 나도 너를 죽여야겠다. 하지만, 만약 열두 시가 되기 전에 산 속 절에 있는 종이 세 번 울리면 너를 살려 주겠다."

큰 뱀이 말했습니다. 그때는 아주 깊은 밤이라 산 속에 아무도 없었고, 열두 시까지 시간이 얼마 남지 않았습니다. 총각은 자신이 죽을 것이라고 생각했습니다. 그때, 종이 세 번 울렸습니다. 뱀이 총각을 풀어 주었습니다.

다음 날 아침 절에 가 보니 까치가 머리에 피를 흘리며 죽어 있고, 종에도 피가 묻어 있었습니다. 총각은 까치를 잘 묻어 주었습니다.

❖ ❖ ❖

The Magpie That Repaid Kindness

❖   This story is about a kind man and a magpie.   ❖

Once upon a time, a young man was going to a village that was across the mountain. As he traveled, he saw a big snake climbing up a tree to prey on a magpie. To help the magpie, the young man shot an arrow and killed the snake. After that, it became nighttime, but the young man was still on the mountain. He found a house on the mountain and decided to go in. The owner of the house was a woman. The young man fell asleep right after eating dinner because he was so tired. He woke up finding it hard to breathe, and discovered a big snake coiled around his body.

"The snake you shot an arrow at and killed was my husband. You killed my husband, so I am going to kill you! Only if the bell at the temple on the mountain rings three times before midnight, will I let you go," said the big snake.

It was then already very late at night. There was no one on the mountain, and there was not much time left before midnight. The young man thought he was going to die. Then, the bell rang three times, and so the snake let him go. The next morning the man went up to the temple, and found the magpie from the day before dead, with blood on his head. There was also blood on the bell. The young man carefully buried the magpie.

❖ ❖ ❖

Pre-Reading Questions (answer in Korean or English)
a. 어떤 사건이 설명되거나 묘사될 것이라고 생각합니까?
b. 이 이야기에서 중요한 물건이나 등장인물을 추측할 수 있습니까?
c. 제목과 부제목이 주는 이 이야기에 대한 단서는 무엇입니까?

Vocabulary

은혜 **eunhye** kindness

갚다 **gapda** to repay

까치 **kkachi** a magpie

산 너머 마을 **san neomeo ma-eul** a village across a mountain

길 **gil** a street

뱀 **baem** a snake

마리 **mali** counter noun for animals

잡아먹다 **jab-ameogda** to prey on

돕다 **dobda** to help

활 **hwal** a bow

쏘다 **ssoda** to shoot

그리고 나서 **geuligo naseo** after that

주인 **ju-in** an owner

숨이 막히다 **sum-i maghida** to be hard to breathe

내 **nae** my

남편 **nampyeon** a husband

만약 **man-yag** if

열두 시 **yeoldu si** 12 o'clock

전에 **jeon-e** before

절 **jeol** a temple

종 **jong** a bell

세 번 **se beon** three times

울리다 **ullida** to ring

살려 주다 **sallyeo juda** to spare one's life

깊은 밤 **gip-eun bam** to be late into the night

피를 흘리다 **pileul heullida** to bleed

묻다 **mudda** to bury/be stained with

Culture Notes

From the old days, a **kkachi** (magpie) was believed to bring good luck. Proverbs involving magpies include, "When a magpie cries in the morning, a pleasant guest will arrive," "When a magpie cries in the morning, something good happens; when it cries in the evening, something bad happens." Unlike magpies, crows were believed to be ominous animals.

Comprehension Questions

a. 총각은 까치를 어떻게 도와 주었습니까?

b. 뱀은 총각이 어떻게 하면 살려 준다고 했습니까?

c. 까치는 총각을 어떻게 살려 주었습니까?

Writing Activity

명함 크기의 종이에 가장 흥미진진한 방식으로 이 이야기를 다시 써 보십시오. 반 친구들과 그 이야기를 같이 읽으십시오. 왜 그것들을 당신의 이야기에 넣었습니까? 당신의 이야기는 다른 친구들의 이야기와 같습니까?

Rewrite the story in the most exciting way you can, on paper the size of a business card. Share it with the class. Why did you include what you did? Does your story match the other students' stories?

구렁이 선비

Guleong-i Seonbi

옛날 옛날에 한 여자가 아들을 낳았는데, 그 아들은 사람이 아니라 구렁이었습니다. 그 여자는 구렁이가 너무 징그러워서 방에서 키우지 못했습니다. 대신 구렁이를 부엌 구석에서 키우고, 망태기를 덮어 놓았습니다. 구렁이는 망태기 안에 누워 있다가 밥을 먹을 시간이 되면 밥을 먹고 다시 망태기 안으로 들어갔습니다.

그 여자의 이웃집에는 세 자매가 살았습니다. 어느 날, 세 딸들이 구렁이를 구경하러 그 여자의 집에 놀러 왔습니다. 첫째딸이 구렁이를 보고, "아이구, 징그러워." 하면서 막대기로 구렁이의 왼쪽 눈을 쿡쿡 찔렀습니다. 그 다음, 둘째딸이 구렁이를 보고, "아이구, 더러워." 하면서 막대기로 구렁이의 오른쪽 눈을 쿡쿡 찔렀습니다. 구렁이의 눈에서 눈물이 흘렀습니다. 셋째딸이 울고 있는 구렁이를 보고, "불쌍하다, 가엾다." 하면서 옷으로 구렁이의 눈물을 닦아 주었습니다.

그러고 나서 구렁이가 자기 어머니에게 "이웃집 셋째딸과 결혼하게 해 주세요." 라고 말했습니다. 어머니가 깜짝 놀라서, "말도 안 되는 소리 하지 마라. 누가 구렁이와 결혼하고 싶어하겠니?" 하고 말했습니다. 하지만 구렁이는 계속 셋째딸과 결혼하게 해 달라고 말했습니다.

"가서 말이라도 한 번 해 보세요. 안 그러면 저 아궁이에 들어가서 다시는 안 나올 거예요." 구렁이 어머니는 할 수 없이 이웃집에 찾아가서 옆집 딸들의 어머니에게 구렁이 아들이 딸과 결혼하고 싶어한다고 말했습니다. 옆집 딸들의 어머니는 화를 냈습니다. 하지만 구렁이 어머니는 딸들에게 한번 물어나 보자고 애원했습니다.

첫째딸에게 구렁이와 결혼하겠냐고 물어 보니까, 첫째딸이 "아이구, 누가 그 징그러운 것과 결혼을 해요?" 하고 화를 냈습니다. 둘째딸에게 구렁이와 결혼하겠냐고 물어 보니까, 둘째딸이 "아이구, 누가 그 더러운 것과 결혼을 해요?" 하고 화를 냈습니다. 마지막으로 셋째딸에게 구렁이와 결혼하겠냐고 물어 보니까, "어머니만 허락해 주시면 결혼하겠습니다." 라고 했습니다. 그래서 구렁이와 셋째딸은 결혼을 하게 되었습니다. 결혼을 하는 날, 구렁이는 옷을 잘 차려 입고 결혼을 했습니다. 결혼

The Rat-Snake Scholar

❖ This story is about a snake-man and his wife. ❖

Once upon a time, a woman gave birth to a son, but her son was a rat snake rather than a human. The woman could not stand to raise the rat snake with her in her room because it was too disgusting, so she raised him in the kitchen corner, covering him with a net bag. The rat snake lay in the net bag, and would come out to eat rice when it was time to eat. He would then go back to his net bag.

There were three sisters who lived next to the woman and the rat snake. One day, the three daughters visited the woman's house to see the rat snake.

The first daughter looked at the rat snake, poked at his left eye with a stick, and said, "Oh, it's so gross!"

Then, the second daughter looked at the rat snake, poked at his right eye with a stick, and said, "Oh, it is so dirty!"

Tears fell from the rat snake's eyes. The third daughter saw the rat snake crying, wiped away his tears with a cloth, and said, "You pitiful and poor thing."

After this, the rat snake said to his mother, "Please let me marry the third daughter."

The mother was surprised and said, "Don't talk such nonsense! Who'd want to marry a rat snake?"

However, the rat snake kept begging his mother to let him marry the third daughter: "Please go and just ask once. If you don't, I will go into the fireplace and never come out again."

His mother obliged. She went to the neighbor's house and said to the girls' mother that her rat-snake son wanted to marry one of her daughters. The girls' mother became angry. However, the rat snake's mother begged her to just ask the daughters and give him a chance.

When she asked the first daughter to marry the rat snake, the first daughter got angry and said, "Oh, who would want to marry the gross thing?"

When she asked the second daughter to marry the rat snake, the second daughter became angry too and said, "Oh, who would want to marry that dirty thing?"

Last, when she asked the third daughter to marry the rat snake, she answered saying, "If my mother will allow it, I would marry him."

식을 마치고 밤이 되자, 구렁이는 뜨거운 물에 목욕을 한 다음, 뱀 허물을 벗고 아주 잘생기고 멋진 선비가 되었습니다. 이웃집 어머니는 셋째 딸을 구렁이와 결혼시켜서 슬퍼했지만, 다음날 아침 아주 잘생긴 구렁이 선비를 보고 아주 놀라고 좋아했습니다. 첫째딸과 둘째딸은 구렁이 선비를 셋째딸에게 빼앗겨서 아주 배가 아팠습니다.

구렁이 선비와 셋째딸은 행복하게 잘 살았습니다. 그러던 어느 날, 구렁이 선비는 과거 시험을 보러 가게 되었습니다. 과거 시험을 보러 가기 전날 저녁에, 구렁이 선비는 자기가 벗고 나왔던 허물을 셋째딸에게 주면서 말했습니다.

"이 허물을 아무한테도 보이지 말고 잘 가지고 있으세요. 이것이 없으면 제가 돌아올 수 없습니다."

셋째딸은 알았다고 했습니다. 구렁이 선비는 다음날 아침 일찍 과거 시험을 보러 떠났습니다. 셋째딸은 허물을 비단 주머니에 넣어서 옷에 매달고 다녔습니다. 어느 날, 언니들이 와서 비단 주머니에 무엇이 있는지 보여 달라고 했습니다. 셋째딸은 보여 주고 싶지 않다고 했지만, 언니들이 억지로 빼앗아서 열어 보고, "아이구, 징그럽고 더러워! 이런 걸 왜 가지고 다니니?" 하며 허물을 불 속에 던져 버렸습니다. 허물은 홀랑 타 버렸습니다. 그래서 구렁이 선비는 돌아오지 않았습니다. 한 달이 지나고 두 달이 지나도, 한 해가 가고 두 해가 가도 돌아오지 않았습니다.

그래서 셋째딸은 구렁이 선비를 찾으러 갔습니다. 계속 계속 걷다가 까마귀 떼를 만났습니다.

"까마귀들아, 구렁이 선비님을 보았니?"

셋째딸이 물었습니다.

"여기 있는 벌레들을 윗물에 씻고 아랫물에 씻고 새하얗게 만들어 주면 알려 주지." 까마귀 떼들이 말했습니다. 그래서 셋째딸은 벌레들을 윗물에 씻고 아랫물에 씻고 새하얗게 만들어 주었습니다. 그랬더니 까마귀들이, "저기로 가서 멧돼지한테 물어 보면 알게 될 거야." 라고 했습니다.

그래서 셋째딸은 또 계속 계속 걷다가 멧돼지를 만났습니다. "멧돼지야, 구렁이 선비님을 보았니?"

셋째딸이 물었습니다.

"여기 있는 칡뿌리를 캐서 흙을 깨끗하게 털고 껍질을 벗겨 주면 알려 주지."

Therefore, the rat snake and the third daughter agreed to get married. On the wedding day, the rat snake got dressed up for the marriage. Then, that night after the wedding ceremony, he took a bath in hot water. As he slipped into the water he slipped out of his snakeskin, and became a very handsome and cool scholar. The mother in the neighboring house had been sad because her third daughter had married a rat snake. However, when she saw this very handsome scholar the next morning, she was very surprised and happy. The first daughter and second daughter felt envious because they lost the chance to be with the scholar.

The scholar and the third daughter lived happily together. Then one day, the scholar was preparing to take the civil service exam. On the evening before going to take the civil service exam, he gave his wife the snakeskin he had slipped out of and said, "Do not show this snakeskin to anyone, and keep good care of it. I cannot come back without it." The third daughter agreed that she would do this. The scholar left early the next morning to take the civil service exam. The third daughter put the snakeskin in a silk pocket and hung it on her clothes. One day, her older sisters came and told her to show them what was in her silk pocket.

The third daughter said she did not want to show them, but her older sisters took the pocket against her will and opened it, saying, "Oh, it is gross and dirty! Why are you carrying this kind of thing?"

They threw the skin into the fire, and it was completely burned. Thus, the scholar did not come back. He did not come back after one month or two months, and even after one or two years.

The third daughter went to find the scholar. As she was walking, she met a flock of crows.

"Crows, did you see the rat-snake scholar?" the third daughter asked.

The flock of crows responded, "We'll let you know if you wash these bugs in the water of the upper stream, and then in the water of lower stream, to make them snowy-white."

So the third daughter washed the bugs in the water of the upper stream, and then in the water of lower stream, and made them snowy white.

Then the crows said, "Go over there, ask the boar, and then you will see."

Thus, continuing on her walk, the third daughter met a boar. "Boar, did you see the rat-snake scholar?" the third daughter asked.

멧돼지가 말했습니다. 그래서 셋째딸은 칡뿌리를 캐서 흙을 깨끗하게 털고 껍질을 벗겨 주었습니다. 그랬더니 멧돼지가, "저기로 가서 빨래하는 할머니한테 물어 보면 알게 될 거야." 라고 했습니다.

그래서 셋째딸은 또 계속 계속 걷다가 빨래하는 할머니를 만났습니다. "할머니, 구렁이 선비님을 보셨나요?"

셋째딸이 물었습니다.

"여기 있는 검은 빨래를 하얗게 하고 하얀 빨래는 검게 빨아서, 맑은 물에 헹구고 보송보송하게 말려 주면 알려 주지."

할머니가 말했습니다. 그래서 셋째딸은 검은 빨래를 하얗게 빨고 하얀 빨래는 검게 빨아서, 맑은 물에 헹구고 보송보송하게 말려 주었습니다. 그랬더니 할머니가 밥그릇 뚜껑과 젓가락 하나를 주면서, "이 밥그릇 뚜껑을 타고 이 젓가락으로 노를 저어 가면 구렁이 선비가 사는 집을 찾을 수 있지." 라고 했습니다.

셋째딸은 밥그릇 뚜껑을 타고 젓가락으로 노를 저어 구렁이 선비의 집에 도착했습니다. 도착하자 이미 밤이 되었습니다. 구렁이 선비는 달을 보며, "달도 밝고 별도 밝은데 내 마음이 외롭구나. 내 아내도 저 달을 보고 있을까." 하고 노래를 하고 있었습니다. 셋째딸도 노래를 불렀습니다. "달도 밝고 별도 밝은데 내 몸이 피곤하구나. 내 남편도 저 달을 보고 있을까." 구렁이 선비가 그 노래를 듣고 뛰어나와서 셋째딸을 껴안았습니다. 셋째딸과 구렁이 선비는 행복하게 살았습니다.

"I'll let you know if you lift this kudzu root, clean the earth away from it, and peel it."

The third daughter lifted the kudzu root, cleaned the earth away from it, and peeled it.

Then, the boar said, "Go over there and ask that old woman who is doing the laundry, then you will see."

As she continued walking, the third daughter met an old woman who was doing the laundry. "Grandmother, did you see the rat-snake scholar?" the third daughter asked.

"I'll let you know if you wash this black laundry until it is white, then wash this white laundry until it is black, and then rinse the laundry with clear water and dry it to make it fluffy."

The third daughter washed the black laundry until it was white, then washed the white laundry until it was black, and then rinsed it with clear water and dried it to make it fluffy.

Then, the old woman gave her the lid of a rice bowl and a pair of chopsticks and said, "If you ride down the river on this lid and row with these chopsticks, then you can find the house where the rat-snake scholar lives."

The third daughter rode on the lid of the rice bowl and rowed with the chopsticks, and arrived at the rat-snake scholar's house. It was already nighttime when she got there.

The rat-snake scholar was looking at the moon and singing, "The moon is bright and the stars are bright too, but I feel lonely. Is my wife looking at the moon too?"

The third daughter then sang, "The moon is bright and the stars are bright too, but I feel tired. Is my husband looking at the moon too?"

The rat-snake scholar heard the song, ran out, and hugged the third daughter. The third daughter and the rat-snake scholar lived happily ever after.

❖ ❖ ❖

Pre-Reading Questions (answer in Korean or English)

a. 어떤 사건이 설명되거나 묘사될 것이라고 생각합니까?

b. 전래동화에서 뱀의 공통적인 성격은 무엇입니까?

c. 뱀과 결혼하는 것에 대해서 어떻게 생각합니까? 그것을 할 수 있다고/없다고 생각합니까? 왜 그렇게 생각합니까?

Vocabulary

구렁이 **guleong-i** a rat snake

선비 **seonbi** a scholar

징그럽다 **jing-geuleobda** to be gross

구석 **guseog** a corner

자매 **jamae** sisters

구경 **gugyeong** a sightseeing trip

쿡쿡 찌르다 **kugkug jjileuda** to poke

눈물 **nunmul** the tears

가엾다 **gayeobsda** to be pitiful

닦아 주다 **dakk-a juda** to wipe away

결혼하고 싶다 **gyeolhonhago sipda** to want to marry

아궁이 **agung-i** a fireplace

허락 **heolag** an approval, permission

옷 **os** clothes

잘 차려 입다 **jal chalyeo ibda** to dress up well

멋지다 **meosjida** to be cool

배가 아프다 **baega apeuda** to feel envious. (It literally means "to have a stomachache," but it also has a meaning of "feeling envious" as an idiom—the latter meaning is used in this folktale.)

과거 시험 **gwageo siheom** a civil service exam

허물 **heomul** a snakeskin

비단 **bidan** silk (fabric)

억지로 **eogjilo** to be against one's will

까마귀 **kkamagwi** a crow

벌레 **beolle** a bug

멧돼지 **mesdwaeji** a boar

빨래 **ppallae** laundry

젓가락 **jeosgalag** chopsticks

노를 젓다 **noleul jeosda** to row

Culture Notes

Imperial exams were civil service examinations to select candidates for the state bureaucracy. These exams were started in the Josun Dynasty. They were only held once every three years, and had many stages, such as pre-exams, the main exam, and another oral exam in front of the king.

Comprehension Questions

a. 셋째딸과 다른 딸들이 구렁이 선비를 대하는 것이 어떻게 달랐습니까?
b. 왜 구렁이 선비는 셋째딸에게 자기의 허물을 가지고 있으라고 말했습니까?
c. 셋째딸이 구렁이 선비를 찾기 위해 해야 했던 일들은 무엇이었습니까?

Writing Activity

이 이야기의 사건들을 순서대로 표시하세요. 화이트보드에 포스트잇을 사용해서사건의 순서를 표시하십시오. 다른 학생들이 표시한 순서와 일치합니까?
Create a timeline that shows the events in the story. Try using Post-it notes on the whiteboard to show the timeline. Does your timeline match others'?

은혜 갚은 두꺼비

Eunhye Gap-eun Dukkeobi

옛날 옛날에 한 가난한 처녀가 있었습니다. 어느 날, 그 처녀가 부엌에서 밥을 푸고 있는데 두꺼비 한 마리가 엉금엉금 기어들어왔습니다. 두꺼비는 처녀를 한 번 쳐다보고 또 밥을 한 번 쳐다봤습니다.

"배가 고파서 밥을 얻어먹으러 왔나 보다. 아이구, 불쌍해라."

처녀는 생각했습니다. 처녀는 밥 한 주걱을 밥그릇에 담아 두꺼비에게 주었습니다. 두꺼비는 밥을 다 먹고 다시 엉금엉금 기어나갔습니다.

그 다음부터 두꺼비는 밥을 먹을 때가 되면 부엌으로 기어들어와 밥을 먹고 갔습니다. 처녀는 두꺼비를 위해 밥을 한 주걱씩 더 했고, 두꺼비는 그 밥을 먹고 점점 커졌습니다. 그러던 어느 날, 마을에 전염병이 돌기 시작했습니다. 사람들은 여자 한 명을 산에 사는 신에게 바쳐야 한다고 생각했습니다. 가난한 처녀는 자기가 신에게 바쳐지고, 돈을 많이 받아서 자기 아버지에게 주기로 했습니다. 처녀가 산으로 가기 전날 저녁, 두꺼비가 또 밥을 얻어먹으러 왔습니다. 처녀는 밥을 많이 퍼 주면서, "두꺼비야 두꺼비야, 이제 내가 죽고 나면 누가 너한테 밥을 주니? 이 밥을 많이 먹고 잘 살아라." 라고 말했습니다. 두꺼비도 그 말을 알아들었는지 눈물을 뚝뚝 흘렸습니다.

다음날 아침, 처녀가 산으로 갔습니다. 그런데 두꺼비도 처녀의 뒤를 따라갔습니다. "두꺼비야 두꺼비야, 따라오면 너도 죽는다. 다시 돌아가라."

처녀가 말했습니다. 하지만 두꺼비는 계속 처녀의 뒤를 따라갔습니다. 처녀가 멈추면 두꺼비도 멈추고, 처녀가 걸으면 두꺼비도 따라 걸었습니다. 마침내 처녀는 산 속 절에 도착했습니다. 처녀가 방에 앉자 두꺼비도 그 옆에 따라 앉았습니다. 밤이 되자 천장에서 이상한 소리가 들렸습니다. 처녀가 위를 보자 아주 큰 왕지네가 천장에서 처녀의 머리를 물려고 하고 있었습니다. 그때 두꺼비가 펄쩍 뛰어올라 지네를 쫓아 버렸습니다.

다음날 아침, 사람들이 처녀의 시체를 치우려고 산 속 절로 왔습니다. 처녀가 살아 있는 것을 보고 다들 깜짝 놀랐습니다. 처녀는 천장에 왕지

The Toad That Repaid Kindness

❖ This story is about a kind girl and a toad. ❖

Once upon a time, there was a poor girl. One day, while the girl was scooping rice, a toad crawled into the kitchen. The toad looked at the girl once, and looked at the rice once.

"Maybe it came here to beg for food because it is hungry. Oh, poor thing!" the girl thought. The girl put a scoop of rice in a bowl and gave it to the toad. The toad crawled out of the kitchen after eating all the rice.

From then on, the toad would crawl into the kitchen when it was time to eat, eat the rice, and then leave. Every day, the girl cooked an additional scoop of rice for the toad, and as the toad ate the rice, it got bigger and bigger. One day, an infectious disease took over the village. The people thought they would have to slay a girl as a tribute to the god on the mountain. The poor girl decided to be the sacrifice to the mountain god, because her father would be paid a lot of money. The evening before the girl was to go to the mountain, the toad came to beg for rice again.

Scooping a lot of rice, the girl said, "Toad, toad. Who is going to give you rice after I die? Eat a lot of this rice and live well."

The toad understood her words and began to cry.

The next morning, the girl went to the mountain, but the toad followed after.

"Toad, toad, you will die too if you follow me. Please return home."

However, the toad kept following the girl. When the girl stopped the toad stopped too, and when the girl walked on, the toad walked on as well. Finally, the girl arrived at the temple on the mountain. She sat down in a room, and the toad sat right next to her. As night fell, they heard a strange sound from the ceiling. When the girl looked up, there was a really big centipede on the ceiling. It was trying to bite the girl's head! In that moment, the toad jumped up and drove the centipede away.

The next morning, people came to the temple on the mountain to prepare the girl's body for burial. They were all surprised when they saw that the girl was still alive. The girl told them about the big centipede in the ceiling. When the people removed the ceiling, the big centipede was still hanging there. Its body was very red because it had sucked up people's blood. The infectious disease had been

네가 있다고 알려 주었습니다. 사람들이 천장을 뜯어내자, 왕지네가 매달려 있었습니다. 왕지네의 몸은 사람들의 피를 빨아먹어서 새빨갰습니다. 전염병은 왕지네 때문이었던 것입니다. 사람들이 왕지네를 잡아서 불태워 죽였습니다. 그러고 나니 사람들의 병이 다 나았습니다.

처녀는 집으로 돌아왔고, 두꺼비에게 다시 밥을 해 주며 아버지와 함께 행복하게 살았습니다.

❖ ❖ ❖

Pre-Reading Questions (answer in Korean or English)
a. 이 이야기에서 중요한 물건이나 등장인물을 추측할 수 있습니까?
b. 제목이 주는 이 이야기에 대한 단서는 무엇입니까?
c. 두꺼비와 관련된 다른 전래 동화를 알고 있습니까? 그 동화에 대해서 간단히 설명할 수 있습니까?

Vocabulary

두꺼비 **dukkeobi** a toad
부엌 **bueok** a kitchen
밥을 푸다 **bab-eul puda** to scoop rice
엉금엉금 **eong-geum-eong-geum** to crawl
기어들어오다 **gieodeul-eooda** to crawl into
쳐다보다 **chyeodaboda** to look
아이구 **aigu** oh, oops
불쌍하다 **bulssanghada** to be pathetic
한 주걱 **han jugeog** one scoop
밥그릇 **babgeuleus** a rice bowl
그 다음부터 **geu da-eumbuteo** from then on
점점 커지다 **jeomjeom keojida** to get bigger and bigger
그러던 어느 날 **geuleodeon eoneu nal** then one day
전염병 **jeon-yeombyeong** an infectious disease

여자 **yeoja** a woman
신 **sin** the god
바치다 **bachida** to offer (a sacrifice)
바쳐지다 **bachyeojida** to be offered (as a sacrifice)
전날 저녁 **jeonnal jeonyeog** the evening before
멈추다 **meomchuda** to stop
마침내 **machimnae** finally
천장 **cheonjang** a ceiling
지네 **jine** a centipede
왕지네 **wangjine** a big centipede
뛰어오르다 **ttwieooleuda** to jump up
쫓아 버리다 **jjoch-a beolida** to drive away
불태워 죽이다 **bultaewo jug-ida** to burn to death

caused by the centipede. The people captured the big centipede, and burned it to death. Consequently, their illness was completely cured and disappeared. The girl came back to her home, cooked rice for the toad again, and lived happily ever after with her father.

⚘ ⚘ ⚘

Culture Notes

A Korean proverb goes, "An enemy should be engraved in water, and a favor should be engraved on a rock." This means an enemy should be forgotten, and a favor should be returned and not forgotten. Traditionally, people considered returning a favor of utmost importance, and there are many Korean folktales with animals who repaid favors.

Comprehension Questions

a. 처녀는 두꺼비를 위해 무엇을 했습니까?
b. 왜 처녀는 산에 사는 신에게 바쳐지기로 했습니까?
c. 산에는 무엇이 있었습니까? 두꺼비는 처녀에게 어떻게 은혜를 갚았습니까?

Writing Activity

이 이야기에 나오는 한 등장인물의 독백을 만드십시오. 그들은 주어진 순간마다 어떤 생각을 하고 무엇을 느낍니까? 왜 그렇습니까?

Create a monologue for a character in the story. What are they thinking/feeling at a certain moment? Why?

정신없는 도깨비

Jeongsin-eomneun Dokkaebi

옛날 옛날에 한 아이가 살았습니다. 아이가 태어나자마자 아이의 부모님이 돌아가셔서, 아이는 아주 가난하고 외로웠습니다. 어느 날, 아이가 이웃 마을에 가서 일하고 돌아오는 길에 산 속에서 제 또래의 꼬마를 만났습니다.

"김 서방아, 김 서방아."

그 꼬마가 아이를 부르고 손뼉을 짝짝 쳤습니다. 그 꼬마는 도깨비였던 것입니다. 도깨비는 사람을 만나면 김 서방이라고 두 번 부르고 손뼉을 치기 때문입니다.

아이는 도깨비를 만나 깜짝 놀랐습니다. 하지만 도깨비를 보고 놀라면 도깨비들이 기분이 나빠져서 심술을 부리기 때문에, 아이는 아무렇지도 않은 척 했습니다.

"왜 불러?"

아이가 물었습니다.

"내가 지금 돈이 없으니까, 딱 서 푼만 빌려 줘라."

도깨비가 말했습니다. 아이가 가진 돈이 딱 서 푼밖에 없었습니다. 그래도 이 돈을 주지 않으면 도깨비가 심술을 부릴 것이 분명했습니다. 그래서 아이는 돈을 빌려 주면서, "이 돈 꼭 갚을 거지?" 하고 물었습니다.

"당연하지. 내일 저녁에 꼭 갚을 테니까 걱정 마라."

도깨비는 그렇게 말하고 연기처럼 사라졌습니다. 아이는 돈이 없어서 그날 저녁을 쫄쫄 굶었습니다.

그 다음날도 아이가 다른 집에 가서 일을 해 주고 집에 왔는데, 밖에서 누가 "김 서방아, 김 서방아." 하고 부른 다음 손뼉을 짝짝 쳤습니다. 아이가 밖에 나가 보니 어제 만난 도깨비가 돈 서 푼을 가지고 왔습니다.

"어제 빌린 서 푼 갚으러 왔다. 여기 있다."

도깨비는 아이에게 서 푼을 주고 다시 연기처럼 사라졌습니다.

그런데, 그 다음 날 저녁에도 집 밖에서 누가 "김 서방아, 김 서방아." 하고 아이를 불렀습니다. 나가 보니 그 도깨비가 또 와 있었습니다.

"어제 빌린 서 푼 갚으러 왔다. 여기 있다."

The Manic Goblin

❧ *This story is about a forgetful goblin.* ❧

Once upon a time, there was a child. The child was very poor and lonely because his parents died right after he was born. One day, the child went to the neighboring town to work, and met a little boy about his age on his way back home over the mountain.

"Mr. Kim! Mr. Kim!" the little boy called after the child, clapping his hands twice. The little boy was a goblin. When goblins meet a person, they call out "Mr. Kim!" twice, and clap their hands.

The child was very surprised to meet the goblin. However, if you show surprise when seeing goblins, the goblins feel bad and will do something mean. So, the child pretended to be calm.

"Why did you call me?" he asked.

The goblin responded, "I do not have money right now, so please lend me some—just three pennies."

The child only had three pennies. However, if he did not give him this money, it was clear that the goblin would do something mean to him. So, the child gave the goblin the money and said, "You're sure to pay back this money, right?"

"Of course. I'll pay you back tomorrow evening, so don't worry," the goblin said. He then disappeared without a trace.

Now without money, the child had to skip dinner.

The next day, the child went to another house to work. After he returned home, somebody called him saying, "Mr. Kim! Mr. Kim!" clapping twice. When the child went outside, the goblin he had met yesterday came to him with three pennies.

"I came here to pay back the three pennies I borrowed yesterday. Here they are." The goblin gave the child the three pennies, and again disappeared without a trace.

The next evening, someone called the child outside saying, "Mr. Kim! Mr. Kim!" When he went out, the goblin was there again.

"I came here to pay you back the three pennies I borrowed yesterday. Here they are." The goblin gave him the three pennies again.

도깨비가 또 서 푼을 주었습니다. 아이가 "빌린 돈은 어제 갚았는데?" 라고 하자, 도깨비가 "내가 언제 갚았어? 어제 너한테 서 푼을 빌리고 오늘 처음 만나는데 언제 갚아?" 라고 하며 사라졌습니다. 도깨비는 이렇게 무엇이든 잘 잊어버리는 것입니다. 아이는 공짜로 돈이 또 생겨서 좋아했습니다.

그런데, 그 다음 날 저녁에도 집 밖에서 누가 "김 서방아, 김 서방아." 하고 아이를 불렀습니다. 나가 보니 그 도깨비가 또 와 있었습니다. "어제 빌린 서 푼 갚으러 왔다. 여기 있다."

도깨비가 또 서 푼을 주었습니다. 그 다음부터 도깨비는 매일 저녁에 와서 돈을 서 푼씩 주고 갔습니다. 아이는 아주 부자가 되었습니다.

그렇게 몇 달이 지났습니다. 어느 날, 도깨비가 돈 갚으러 와서 "나 너희 집에서 좀 놀다 가면 안 될까?" 하고 물어 보았습니다. 아이는 도깨비에게 들어오라고 했습니다. 아이의 집에서 놀던 도깨비는 다 찌그러진 냄비 하나를 보고는, "우리 집에 새 냄비가 하나 있는데 가져다 줄까?" 하고 물었습니다. 아이는 좋다고 했습니다.

그 다음날 저녁, 도깨비가 와서 서 푼과 냄비 하나를 주었습니다. 아이가 도깨비가 준 냄비에 밥을 짓자, 밥을 먹어도 먹어도 밥이 계속 생겼습니다. 도깨비가 요술 냄비를 가져다 준 것입니다. 그 다음 날 저녁은 어땠을까요? 그렇습니다. 도깨비가 다시 찾아와 또 서 푼과 냄비 하나를 주고 갔습니다. 그 다음부터 도깨비는 매일 저녁에 와서 서 푼과 냄비 하나를 주고 갔습니다. 요술 냄비가 많이 생긴 아이는 그 냄비를 마을 사람들에게 하나씩 나누어 주었습니다.

그렇게 또 몇 달이 지났습니다. 어느 날, 도깨비가 돈과 냄비를 주러 와서 "나 너희 집에서 좀 놀다 가면 안 될까?" 하고 물어 보았습니다. 아이는 도깨비에게 들어오라고 했습니다. 아이의 집에서 놀던 도깨비는 작아진 다듬이방망이를 보고, "우리 집에 새 방망이가 하나 있는데 가져다 줄까?" 하고 물었습니다. 아이는 좋다고 했습니다.

그 다음날 저녁, 도깨비가 찾아와서 서 푼과 냄비 하나, 그리고 방망이 하나를 주었습니다. 아이가 방망이를 두드리자, 새 옷, 새 이불, 새 집이 나왔습니다. 도깨비가 원하는 것을 모두 주는 도깨비 방망이를 가져다 준 것입니다. 그 다음 날 저녁에 도깨비가 다시 찾아와 또 서 푼과 냄비 하나, 도깨비 방망이 하나를 주고 갔습니다. 그 다음부터 도깨비는 매

The child asked, "Didn't you already pay back the money you borrowed yesterday?"

The goblin then answered, "When did I pay you back? How could I pay you back since this is the first time I've seen you after I borrowed three pennies from you yesterday?" and disappeared.

As it turns out, goblins are forgetful of things like this. But the child was happy because he got money again for nothing.

The next evening, someone called the child outside saying, "Mr. Kim! Mr. Kim!" When he went out, the goblin had come again. "I came here to pay you back the three pennies I borrowed yesterday. Here they are." The goblin gave him the three pennies again.

After that, the goblin came to his house every evening and gave him three pennies each time. The child became very rich.

A few months later, the goblin came again to pay back the money and asked, "Can I hang out in your house just for a moment?"

The child told the goblin to come in. While hanging out in the child's house, the goblin saw a dented pot and asked, "I have a new pot at home, would you like me to bring it and give it to you?"

The child said, "Yes."

The next evening, the goblin came to give him the three pennies and the pot. When the child cooked rice in the pot that the goblin had given him, rice began continuously pouring from it, because the goblin brought him a magic pot.

Can you guess what happened the next evening? Yes. The goblin came again and gave the child three pennies and another pot. The child received so many magic pots that he gave them away to the people in the town.

One day a few months later, the goblin came to give the child money and a pot, and asked again, "Can I hang out in your house just for a moment?"

The child told the goblin to come in. While in the child's house, the goblin saw a laundry bat, which was becoming smaller and asked, "I have a new bat at home, would you like me to bring it and give it to you?"

The child said, "Yes."

The next evening, the goblin came and gave the child three pennies, a pot, and a bat. When the child beat the bat, new clothes, a new blanket, and a new house came out. It was because the goblin brought a goblin bat, which gives you everything you want.

일 저녁에 와서 서 푼과 냄비 하나, 도깨비 방망이 하나를 주고 갔습니다. 도깨비 방망이가 많이 생긴 아이는 그 방망이를 마을 사람들에게 하나씩 나누어 주었습니다.

어느 날, 아이가 이웃 마을에 놀러 가고 있는데 하늘에서 "김 서방아, 김 서방아." 하고 부른 다음 손뼉을 짝짝 치는 소리가 들렸습니다. 하늘을 보자 도깨비가 나무 위에서 훌쩍 훌쩍 울고 있었습니다.

"왜 거기서 울고 있어?"

아이가 물었습니다.

"내가 죄를 너무 많이 지어서 하늘에 있는 도깨비 왕에게 벌 받으러 가야 돼."

도깨비가 울면서 대답했습니다.

"무슨 죄를 지었어?"

아이가 물었습니다.

"집에 있는 돈이랑 냄비랑 도깨비 방망이를 남한테 너무 많이 줬대. 나는 그러지 않은 것 같은데…"

도깨비가 대답했습니다. 아이는 미안했습니다. 도깨비가 다시 울면서 말했습니다. "내가 지금 벌 받으면 언제 다시 올 지 모르는데, 너한테 빌린 돈 서 푼도 못 갚고, 냄비랑 방망이도 못 주고 가서 미안해. 벌 다 받고 오면 그때 꼭 줄게."

이제까지 아이에게 돈과 냄비, 도깨비 방망이를 가져다 준 것을 잊어버린 것입니다. 도깨비는 하늘로 올라갔고, 그 도깨비를 다시 본 사람은 아무도 없었다고 합니다. 여러분도 도깨비가 돈을 빌려 달라고 하면 꼭 빌려 주세요.

❖ ❖ ❖

The next evening, the goblin came and gave the child three pennies, a pot, and a goblin bat again. After that, the goblin came every evening and gave the child three pennies, a pot, and a goblin bat. The child received so many goblin bats that he gave them to the people in town.

One day, while the child visited a neighboring town, he heard the sound of someone calling from the sky, "Mr. Kim! Mr. Kim!," with two claps. Looking up, he saw the goblin weeping in a tree.

"Why are you crying there?" the child asked.

"I have committed many sins, so I have to be punished by the Goblin King in the sky," the goblin answered with a sob.

"What sin did you commit?" the child asked.

The goblin answered, "I gave away to much money, too many pots, and too many goblin bats to people. I didn't think I had done such a thing ..."

The child felt sorry for him.

The goblin continued crying and said, "I'm on my way to be punished, so I don't know when I will come here again. I am so sorry that I didn't pay back the three pennies I borrowed from you, and that I didn't give you the pot or the bat. If I come back here after my punishment, I will give them to you then."

He had forgotten that he had brought him the money, pots, and goblin bats.

The goblin went up into the sky, and no one ever saw him again.

So, if a goblin asks you for money, you should lend him some!

❖ ❖ ❖

Pre-Reading Questions (answer in Korean or English)
a. 어떤 사건이 설명되거나 묘사될 것이라고 생각합니까?
b. 전래동화에서 도깨비의 공통적인 성격은 무엇입니까?
c. 이 이야기에서 중요한 물건이나 등장인물을 추측할 수 있습니까?

Vocabulary

정신없다 **jeongsin-eobsda** to be manic

도깨비 **dokkaebi** a goblin

태어나자마자 **taeeonajamaja** right after you were born

외롭다 **oelobda** to be lonely

또래 **ttolae** about the same age as

꼬마 **kkoma** a little boy

손뼉을 치다 **sonppyeog-eul chida** to clap

두 번 **du beon** twice

기분이 나빠지다 **gibun-i nappajida** to feel bad

아무렇지 않은 척 **amuleohji anh-eun cheog** to pretend to be calm

돈을 빌리다 **don-eul billida** to lend money

돈을 갚다 **don-eul gapda** to pay back money

쫄쫄 굶다 **jjoljjol gulmda** to skip a meal entirely

연기처럼 사라지다 **yeongicheoleom salajida** to disappear without a trace

공짜로 **gongjjalo** for nothing, for free

몇 달 **myeoch dal** a few months

찌그러지다 **jjigeuleojida** to be dented

냄비 **naembi** a pot

요술 **yosul** magic

다듬이방망이 **dadeum-ibangmang-i** a laundry bat

도깨비 방망이 **dokkaebi bangmang-i** a goblin bat (a magical bat)

두드리다 **dudeulida** to beat

이불 **ibul** a blanket

훌쩍 훌쩍 울다 **huljjeog huljjeog ulda** to weep/shed a few tears

죄 **joe** a sin

벌을 받다 **beol-eul badda** to be punished

이제까지 **ijekkaji** until now

Culture Notes

People used to believe that an object that is thrown away after being used turned into a goblin. Such a goblin likes to sing and dance, and play tricks on people. Goblins have a mysterious power to turn mountains into a plain overnight, but they do not have good memories and are considered naïve. Consequently, they keep repaying their debts over and over again after they borrow money from someone.

Comprehension Questions

a. 어떻게 아이는 도깨비를 만난 것을 알았습니까?
b. 아이가 도깨비에게 받은 세 개의 물건은 무엇이었습니까?
c. 도깨비는 왜 이야기의 마지막에서 울었습니까?

Writing Activity

이 이야기의 도깨비에게 엽서를 쓰세요. 도깨비에게 당신이 그의 성격에 대해서 어떻게 생각하는지, 그리고 도깨비에게 주고 싶은 제안을 들려주세요.

Write a postcard to the goblin in the story. Tell him what you think about his characteristics and what suggestions you want to give to him.

좁쌀 한 알

Jobssal Han Al

옛날 옛날에 한 노총각이 살았습니다. 이 총각은 정말 똑똑하고 착한 사람이었지만, 너무 가난해서 결혼을 하지 못했습니다. 그래서, 결혼할 여자를 구하기 위해 여행을 떠났습니다. 하지만 노총각은 돈이 없었기 때문에 좁쌀 한 알만 가지고 갔습니다. 걷다가 걷다가 밤이 되어서 노총각은 어떤 집에서 자고 가게 되었습니다. 노총각은 집 주인에게 좁쌀 한 알을 맡기며 말했습니다.

"이걸 잘 가지고 있다가 내일 꼭 저에게 돌려주세요."

"네, 알겠어요."

집주인이 대답했습니다. 하지만 주인은 좁쌀 한 알을 보고 그냥 방구석에 던져 놓았습니다. 그런데, 그날 밤 쥐가 그 좁쌀을 먹어 버렸습니다. 다음날 아침, 노총각은 집주인에게 어제 맡긴 좁쌀을 달라고 했지만 집주인은 그 좁쌀을 찾을 수가 없었습니다.

"아마 어젯밤에 쥐가 먹어 버렸나 봐요. 내가 다른 좁쌀을 줄게요."

주인이 말했습니다.

"안돼요, 안돼요. 꼭 그 좁쌀이어야 해요."

노총각이 말했습니다.

"쥐가 먹어 버린 좁쌀을 어떻게 찾아요?" 주인이 당황했습니다.

"그러면 제 좁쌀을 먹은 쥐를 잡아 주세요."

노총각이 말했습니다. 그래서 집주인은 그 쥐를 잡아다 주었습니다. 노총각은 그 쥐를 가지고 다시 여행을 떠났습니다.

걷다가 걷다가 밤이 되어서 노총각은 또 어떤 집에서 자고 가게 되었습니다. 노총각은 집 주인에게 쥐를 맡기며 말했습니다.

"이 쥐를 잘 가지고 있다가 내일 꼭 저에게 돌려주세요."

"네, 알겠어요."

집주인이 대답했습니다. 주인은 쥐를 주머니에 넣어 부엌에 놓았습니다. 그런데, 그날 밤 고양이가 그 쥐를 먹어 버렸습니다. 다음날 아침, 노총각은 집주인에게 어제 맡긴 쥐를 달라고 했지만 집주인은 그 쥐를 찾을 수 없었습니다.

A Single Grain of Millet

❖   *This story is about an old bachelor and his marriage.*   ❖

Once upon a time, there was an old bachelor. This old bachelor was really smart and nice, but he could not marry because he was too poor. So, in order to find a woman who would marry him, he went off on a journey. Because he did not have money, he brought just a single grain of millet. As he walked on and on, it became night, so the old bachelor decided to stay at a house.

The old bachelor entrusted the single grain of millet to the owner of the house and said, "Please take care of it carefully, and give it back to me tomorrow."

The owner of the house answered, "Okay, I see."

However, he took the single grain of the millet and just threw it in a room. A mouse ate the millet grain that night. The next morning, the old bachelor asked the owner of the house to return him the millet grain that he deposited with him the day before, but the owner of the house could not find it.

The owner said, "Maybe a mouse ate it last night. I will give you another millet grain."

The old bachelor replied, "No! No! It should be that millet grain."

The embarrassed owner answered, "How can I find a millet grain a mouse ate?"

The old bachelor responded, "Then please catch the mouse that ate my millet grain."

So the owner of the house caught the mouse and gave it to him. The old bachelor went off again on his journey with the mouse.

As he walked on and on, it became night, so the old bachelor stayed at another house. The old bachelor gave the mouse to the owner of the house and said, "Please take care of this mouse carefully, and give it back to me tomorrow."

"Okay, I see," the owner of the house answered.

The owner put the mouse in his pocket, and later let it free in the kitchen. A cat ate the mouse that night. The next morning, the old bachelor asked the owner of the house for the mouse that he had given him the previous day, but the owner of the house could not find it.

"Maybe our cat ate it last night. I will catch another mouse and give it to you," the owner said.

"아마 어젯밤에 우리 집 고양이가 먹어 버렸나 봐요. 내가 다른 쥐를 잡아 줄게요."

주인이 말했습니다.

"안돼요, 안돼요. 꼭 그 쥐여야 해요."

노총각이 말했습니다.

"고양이가 먹어 버린 쥐를 어떻게 찾아요?"

주인이 당황했습니다.

"그러면 제 쥐를 먹은 고양이를 주세요."

노총각이 말했습니다. 그래서 집주인은 그 고양이를 주었습니다. 노총각은 그 고양이를 가지고 다시 여행을 떠났습니다.

걷다가 걷다가 밤이 되어서 노총각은 또 어떤 집에서 자고 가게 되었습니다. 노총각은 집 주인에게 고양이를 맡기며 말했습니다.

"이 고양이를 잘 가지고 있다가 내일 꼭 저에게 돌려주세요."

"네, 알겠어요."

집주인이 대답했습니다. 주인은 고양이를 마구간에 묶어 놓았습니다. 그런데, 그날 밤 말이 그 고양이를 밟아 버렸습니다. 다음날 아침, 노총각은 집주인에게 어제 맡긴 고양이를 달라고 했지만 고양이는 죽어 있었습니다.

"아마 어젯밤에 우리 집 말이 밟아 버렸나 봐요. 내가 다른 고양이를 잡아 줄게요."

주인이 말했습니다.

"안돼요, 안돼요. 꼭 그 고양이여야 해요."

노총각이 말했습니다.

"고양이가 이미 죽었는데 어떡해요?"

주인이 당황했습니다.

"그러면 제 고양이를 밟은 말을 주세요."

노총각이 말했습니다. 그래서 집주인은 그 말을 주었습니다. 노총각은 그 말을 가지고 다시 여행을 떠났습니다.

걷다가 걷다가 밤이 되어서 노총각은 또 어떤 집에서 자고 가게 되었습니다. 노총각은 집 주인에게 말을 맡기며 말했습니다.

"이 말을 잘 가지고 있다가 내일 꼭 저에게 돌려주세요."

"네, 알겠어요."

"No! No! It should be the mouse I gave you," the old bachelor said.

"How can I find the mouse that the cat ate?" asked the embarrassed owner.

The old bachelor replied, "Then please give me the cat that ate my mouse."

So, the owner of the house gave him the cat. The old bachelor went off again on his journey with the cat.

As he walked on and on, it became night, so the old bachelor stayed at a house once again. The old bachelor entrusted the cat to the owner of the house and said, "Please take care of this cat carefully and give it back to me tomorrow."

"Okay, I see," the owner of the house answered.

The owner tied up the cat in the horse stable. But that night a horse stomped on the cat. The next morning, the old bachelor asked the owner of the house to give him back the cat that he gave him the day before, but the cat was dead.

"Maybe my horse stomped on it last night. I will catch another cat and give it to you," the owner said.

"No! No! It should be the cat I gave you," the old bachelor answered.

"It's already dead, so what should I do?" The owner was embarrassed.

The old bachelor said, "Then please give me the horse that stomped on my cat."

So, the owner of the house gave the horse to him. The old bachelor went off again on his journey with the horse.

As he walked on and on, it became night, so the old bachelor stayed at a house again. The old bachelor entrusted the horse to the owner of the house and said, "Please take care of this horse carefully and give it back to me tomorrow."

"Okay, I see," the owner of the house answered.

The owner tied the horse in the cow barn, but a cow gored the horse with its horn. The next morning, the old bachelor asked the owner of the house to give back the horse that he had given him the day before, but the horse was dead.

"Maybe my cow gored it with its horn. I will give you another horse," the owner said.

"No! No! It should be that horse," the old bachelor replied.

"It is already dead, so what should I do?" The owner was embarrassed.

The old bachelor said, "Then please give the cow that gored my horse with its horn."

집주인이 대답했습니다. 주인은 말을 외양간에 묶어 놓았습니다. 그런데, 그날 밤 소가 그 말을 뿔로 받아 버렸습니다. 다음날 아침, 노총각은 집주인에게 어제 맡긴 말을 달라고 했지만 말은 죽어 있었습니다.

"아마 어젯밤에 우리 집 소가 뿔로 받아 버렸나 봐요. 내가 다른 말을 줄게요."

주인이 말했습니다.

"안돼요, 안돼요. 꼭 그 말이여야 해요."

노총각이 말했습니다.

"말이 이미 죽었는데 어떡해요?"

주인이 당황했습니다.

"그러면 제 말을 뿔로 받은 소를 주세요."

노총각이 말했습니다. 그래서 집주인은 그 소를 주었습니다. 노총각은 그 소를 가지고 다시 여행을 떠났습니다.

걷다가 걷다가 보니 서울에 도착했습니다. 밤이 되어서 노총각은 또 어떤 집에서 자고 가게 되었습니다. 노총각은 집 주인에게 소를 맡기며 말했습니다.

"이 소를 잘 가지고 있다가 내일 꼭 저에게 돌려주세요."

"네, 알겠어요."

집주인이 대답했습니다. 주인은 소를 외양간에 묶어 놓았습니다. 그런데, 그날 밤 집주인 아들이 소를 데려가서 팔아 버렸습니다. 다음날 아침, 노총각은 집주인에게 어제 맡긴 소를 달라고 했지만 소가 없었습니다.

"아마 어젯밤에 우리 집 아들이 소를 팔아 버렸나 봐요. 내가 다른 소를 줄게요."

주인이 말했습니다.

"안돼요, 안돼요. 꼭 그 소여야 해요."

노총각이 말했습니다.

"이미 팔린 소를 어디에서 찾아요?" 주인이 당황했습니다.

"그러면 제 소를 산 사람을 찾아야겠어요." 노총각이 말했습니다.

노총각은 소 시장에 가서 그 소를 산 사람을 찾아다녔습니다. 어떤 사람이 그 소는 정승의 집으로 팔려 갔다고 했습니다. 오늘이 정승 딸의 생일이라, 생일 잔치에서 소고기를 먹기로 했기 때문입니다. 그래서 노총

So, the owner of the house gave the old bachelor the cow. The old bachelor went off again on his journey with the cow.

As he walked on and on, he arrived in Seoul. It became night again, so the old bachelor stayed at a house again. The old bachelor entrusted the cow to the owner of the house and said, "Please take care of this cow carefully and give it back to me tomorrow."

"Okay, I see," the owner of the house answered.

The owner of the house tied the cow in the cow barn. But, during the night, the owner's son sold the cow. The next morning, the old bachelor asked the owner of the house to return the cow that he had given him the day before, but the cow was gone.

"Maybe my son sold the cow last night. I will give you another cow," the owner said.

"No! No! It should be the cow I gave you," the old bachelor replied.

"It's already sold, where can I find it?" The owner was embarrassed.

The old bachelor said, "Then I will find the person who bought my cow."

The old bachelor looked for the person who bought the cow in the cow market. Someone said that the cow was sold to the minister's household. Since that day was the birthday of the minister's daughter, they had decided to serve beef at the birthday party. Therefore, the old bachelor went to the minister's house and asked the minister to give him back his cow. The servants tried to kick the old bachelor out, but the minister called in the old bachelor and asked him what had happened. So, the old bachelor explained everything that had happened so

각은 정승의 집에 찾아가서 내 소를 달라고 말했습니다. 하인들이 노총각을 내쫓으려고 했지만, 정승이 노총각을 불러 무슨 일이냐고 물었습니다. 그래서 노총각은 이제까지 있었던 일을 설명했습니다. 정승이 들어 보니 좁쌀 한 알이 쥐가 되고, 쥐가 고양이가 되고, 고양이가 말이 되고, 말이 소가 된 이야기였습니다.

"잘 알겠다. 하지만 소는 이미 다 먹어 버렸는데 어떡하지?"

정승이 물었습니다.

"그럼 그 소를 먹은 사람을 주세요."

소를 먹은 사람은 정승의 딸이었습니다. 정승은 화를 내려고 했지만, 노총각을 가만히 보니 똑똑하고 착해 보여서 자기 딸과 결혼을 시키기로 했습니다. 노총각은 좁쌀 한 알로 정승의 딸과 결혼해서 행복하게 살았습니다.

❖ ❖ ❖

Pre-Reading Questions (answer in Korean or English)

a. 좁쌀 한 알과 결혼은 어떤 관련이 있을까요?

b. 제목이 주는 이 이야기에 대한 단서는 무엇입니까?

c. 이 이야기에서 중요한 물건이나 등장인물을 추측할 수 있습니까?

Vocabulary

좁쌀 **jobssal** millet

똑똑하다 **ttogttoghada** to be smart

구하다 **guhada** to find/to seek

여행을 떠나다 **yeohaeng-eul tteo-nada** to go off on a journey

한 알 **han al** a single grain

가지고 있다 **gajigo issda** to take, to have

돌려주다 **dollyeojuda** to give back, return

어젯밤 **eojesbam** last night

다른 **daleun** to be different, another

~이어/아야만 하다 **~ieo/ayaman hada** it should be ~

당황하다 **danghwanghada** to be embarrassed

고양이 **goyang-i** a cat

마구간 **magugan** a horse barn

말 **mal** a horse

밟다 **balbda** to stomp on

외양간 **oeyang-gan** a cow barn

소 **so** a cow

뿔 **ppul** a horn

받다 **badda** to receive/to butt

팔다 **palda** to sell

팔리다 **pallida** to be sold

정승 **jeongseung** a minister

생일 **saeng-il** a birthday

far. The minister listened to it all: How a single grain of millet became a mouse, a mouse became a cat, a cat became a horse, and a horse became a cow.

"I see. However, we already ate the cow, so what should I do?" the minister asked.

The old bachelor answered, "Then please give me the person who ate the cow."

The person who ate the cow was the minister's daughter. The minister was about to become upset, but when he gazed at the old bachelor who looked so smart and nice, he decided to allow him to marry his daughter.

Thus, the old bachelor married the minister's daughter because of a single grain of millet, and they lived happily ever after.

❖ ❖ ❖

생일 잔치 **saeng-il janchi** a birthday party

하인 **hain** a servant

설명하다 **seolmyeonghada** to explain

이미 **imi** already

Culture Notes

A **jeong-seung** (minister) was the highest government position in old Korea. The position can be compared to the prime minister today. Famous ministers were known for living righteously without profiting from their position.

Comprehension Questions

a. 왜 노총각에게 좁쌀 한 알 밖에 없었습니까?

b. 노총각은 어떻게 쥐, 고양이, 말, 그리고 소를 받았습니까?

c. 노총각은 어떻게 정승의 딸과 결혼할 수 있었습니까?

Writing Activity

이 이야기의 사건들을 순서대로 표시하세요. 화이트보드에 포스트잇을 사용해서 사건의 순서를 표시하십시오. 다른 학생들이 표시한 순서와 일치합니까?

Create a timeline that shows the events in the story. Use Post-it notes on the whiteboard to show the timeline. Does your timeline match others'?

삼형제

Samhyeongje

옛날 옛날에 한 남자와 그의 아들 삼형제가 살았습니다. 삼형제가 다 컸을 때, 이 남자가 아파서 죽게 되었습니다. 이 남자는 죽기 전에 삼형제를 불러서 말했습니다.

"내 돈은 모두 불쌍한 사람들에게 줬다. 그래서 너희들에게 줄 것은 이 담뱃대, 맷돌, 장구 세 개 뿐이다. 이 물건들을 나누어 가지고 행복하게 살아라." 이렇게 말하고 이 남자는 죽었습니다.

삼형제는 아버지의 장례식을 치르고 나서 유산 세 가지를 나누어 가졌습니다. 첫째는 나이가 많아서 담뱃대를 가졌고, 둘째는 힘이 세서 맷돌을 가졌고, 막내는 장구를 잘 쳐서 장구를 가졌습니다. 그리고 삼형제는 다른 곳으로 가서 먹고 살기 위해 여행을 떠났습니다. 걷다가 걷다가 세 갈래 길이 나왔습니다. 삼형제는 어디로 갈지 많이 생각했습니다. 첫째가 말했습니다.

"여기서 헤어져서 가고 싶은 길로 갔다가, 돈을 벌면 여기로 다시 돌아와서 집을 짓고 살자. 그러면 우리들이 다시 만날 수 있을 거야."

둘째도 막내도 그러자고 말했습니다. 그래서 첫째는 왼쪽 길로 가고, 둘째는 가운데 길로 가고, 막내는 오른쪽 길로 갔습니다.

첫째는 담뱃대를 가지고 왼쪽 길을 걷고 또 걸었습니다. 첫째가 아직 산 속을 걷고 있는데 그만 밤이 되었습니다. 마침 산 속에 집이 하나 있어서, 첫째가 그 집에 들어가 집주인을 불렀습니다. 그러자 아주 멀리서 여자 목소리가 들렸습니다.

"누구세요?"

그래서 첫째가 대문을 열고 들어가니 또 대문이 있고, 그 대문을 열고 들어가니 또 대문이 있었습니다. 열두 개의 대문을 열고 들어가니 한 여자가 혼자 앉아 있었습니다.

"왜 여기에 혼자 있어요?"

첫째가 물었습니다.

The Three Brothers

❖ *This story is about what happend to three brothers after their father died.* ❖

Once upon a time, there was a man with three sons. After the three brothers had all grown up, the man became sick. The man called the three brothers together before he died and said, "I gave all of my money to poor people. Therefore, the only things I can give you are this pipe, this millstone, and a double-headed drum. Divide these things among yourselves and have a happy life."

The three brothers divided up the three elements of this legacy after their father's funeral. The oldest brother got the pipe because he was older, the second oldest brother got the millstone because he was strong, and the youngest brother got the drum because he was good at playing the *jang-gu*. The three brothers went off on a journey somewhere else, with plans to live in a new place. As they walked and walked, they came to a place where the road divided into three paths. The three brothers thought a lot about where they should go.

The oldest one said, "Let's part from here on, and go down the road each of us wants to go. If we earn any money, then we'll come back here and build a house and live in it together. Then we will be together again."

His brothers agreed. So, the oldest went down the left road, the second oldest went down the middle road, and the youngest went down the right road.

The oldest brother walked and walked with his pipe, down the left road. It became night, and he was still in the mountains. About that time, he saw a house, so he went up to the house and called out to the owner. He heard a woman's voice from very far away saying, "Who is it?" So he opened the main door and went in, and there was a main door again, and as he opened it again and went into it, there was a main door again. After he had opened twelve main doors, he found a woman sitting alone.

"Why are you alone here?" the oldest son asked.

The woman answered, "Originally, my family numbered seven people, but several days ago they died one by one, and I am now alone."

The oldest son was concerned about the woman, so he said, "I'll wait and see what happens tonight. You should hide."

"What if something happens to you?" the woman said worriedly.

"원래 우리 가족은 일곱명이었는데 며칠 전부터 한 사람씩 죽었습니다. 그리고 이제 저 혼자 남았습니다."

여자가 대답했습니다. 첫째는 여자가 걱정됐습니다. 그래서, "오늘 밤에 내가 무슨 일이 일어나는지 볼 테니까 당신은 숨어 있으세요." 라고 말했습니다.

"그러다가 당신한테 무슨 일이라도 생기면 어떡해요?" 여자가 걱정하며 말했습니다.

"걱정하지 마세요."

첫째가 말했습니다. 첫째는 여자를 숨기고 자기가 여자의 옷을 입고 앉아 있었습니다. 조금 후에, 밖에서 바람이 불더니 대문 열두 개가 열리는 소리가 들렸습니다. 그러다가 까만 무엇이 방 안으로 들어와 첫째의 다리를 꽉 잡았습니다.

'아이고, 이제 죽었다. 지금 칼이 있었으면 이걸 죽일 수 있을 텐데.'

첫째가 생각했습니다. 그러다가 주머니에서 담뱃대를 꺼내 담배를 피웠습니다. 첫째가 담배 연기를 뱉자 첫째의 다리를 잡고 있던 것이 기절했습니다. 불을 켜고 봤더니 까맣고 큰 왕지네가 죽어 있었습니다. 아버지가 주신 담뱃대 덕분에 목숨을 건진 것입니다. 첫째는 여자와 결혼해서 다시 갈림길로 돌아와 집을 짓고 살았습니다.

둘째는 맷돌을 가지고 가운데 길을 걷고 또 걸었습니다. 둘째가 아직 산 속을 걷고 있는데 그만 밤이 되었습니다. 마침 산 속에 집이 하나 있어서, 둘째가 그 집에 들어가 집주인을 불렀습니다. 하지만 집에는 아무도 없었습니다. 둘째는 다리도 아프고 졸려서 그 집에서 하루 자고 가기로 했습니다. 누워서 자려고 하는데 밖에서 시끄러운 소리가 들렸습니다. 밖을 보니 키가 아주 큰 사람들이 방망이를 들고 떠들면서 빈 집 쪽으로 오고 있었습니다. '아이구, 일단 숨어야겠다.'

둘째가 생각했습니다. 둘째는 맷돌을 가지고 천장으로 올라가 숨었습니다. 키가 큰 사람들이 방으로 들어와서, "얘들아, 배고픈데 밥이나 먹자." 하고 방망이를 두드렸습니다. 그러자 방망이에서 밥이 나왔습니다.

'저것들이 도깨비들이구나.'

둘째가 생각했습니다. 도깨비들이 밥을 다 먹고 "옷 나와라," 하자 옷이 나왔고, "돈 나와라," 하자 돈이 나왔습니다. 그러고 나서 춤을 추며 밤새 놀았습니다. 조금 후에, 한 도깨비가 냄새를 킁킁 맡았습니다.

"Don't worry about me," the oldest son said.

He hid the woman and sat there wearing the woman's clothes. After a while, wind began to blow outside, and he could hear the sound of the twelve main doors opening. Then something black came into the room and grasped the oldest son's legs.

"Oh, I'm dead! If I had a sword then I could kill this thing," the oldest son thought. He then took the pipe from his pocket and began to smoke. When he exhaled the tobacco smoke, the thing that grasped his legs passed out.

After turning on the lights, he saw a big black centipede lying dead. His life had been saved because of his father's pipe. The oldest son married the woman, came back to the crossroads, built a house and lived there.

The second son walked and walked with the millstone, down the middle road. It became night, and he was still in the mountains. About that time, he saw a house, so he went into the house and called out to the owner. However, no one was there. His legs hurt and he was very sleepy, so he decided to stay for just one night at this house. But when he lay down and tried to sleep, he could hear a noise coming from outside. As he looked outside, there were very tall people coming to the empty house while making noises with bats.

"Oh, I should hide immediately," he thought. He climbed up to the ceiling and hid with the millstone.

The tall people came into the room and said, "Since we are hungry, let's eat some rice."

They then beat their bats, and rice came out from them. After these goblins ate up the rice, they said, "Come out, clothes!" and clothes came out. They then said, "Come out, money!" and money came out. They then began having fun and dancing. This lasted all night.

"인간 냄새가 난다, 인간 냄새가 나."

그 도깨비가 말했습니다. 그러자 다른 도깨비들도 쿵쿵 냄새를 맡더니, "천장에서 인간냄새가 난다," 하며 천장에 올라오려고 했습니다.

"아이고, 이제 죽었다. 지금 칼이 있었으면 저것들을 죽일 수 있을 텐데."

둘째가 생각했습니다. 그러다가 가지고 있던 맷돌을 돌렸습니다. 아무것도 없는 맷돌을 돌려서 소리가 아주 컸습니다. 그러자 도깨비들이 방망이를 던져 버리고 우르르 도망을 갔습니다. 도깨비들은 원래 겁이 많아서, 맷돌 소리가 집이 무너지는 소리인 줄 알았던 것입니다. 둘째가 천장에서 내려와 보니 도깨비 방망이들이 아주 많았습니다. 아버지가 주신 맷돌 덕분에 부자가 된 것입니다. 둘째는 도깨비 방망이를 가지고 다시 갈림길로 돌아와 집을 짓고 살았습니다.

막내는 장구를 가지고 오른쪽 길을 걷고 또 걸었습니다. 막내가 아직 산 속을 걷고 있는데 그만 밤이 되었습니다. 하지만 그 산 속에는 집이 없었습니다. 그래서 여기 저기 돌아다니다 호랑이들을 만났습니다. 호랑이들은 막내를 잡아먹으려고 했습니다. 막내가 한 나무 위로 도망가자, 호랑이들도 목말을 타고 나무 위로 올라오려고 했습니다. "아이고, 이제 죽었다. 지금 칼이 있었으면 저것들을 죽일 수 있을 텐데."

막내가 생각했습니다. 그러다가 가지고 있던 장구를 쳤습니다. 막내는 노래까지 신나게 부르며 장구를 쳤습니다. 그러자 호랑이들이 신이 나서 춤을 추었습니다. 어깨를 으쓱으쓱 거리고, 앞다리를 덜렁덜렁거리고, 뒷다리도 움찔움찔 거리며 춤을 추다가 목말이 무너져서 호랑이들은 다 목이 부러져서 죽었습니다. 막내가 나무에서 내려와서 보니 나무 밑에 죽은 호랑이들이 아주 많았습니다. 막내는 그 호랑이들의 가죽을 벗겨서 비싸게 팔았습니다. 아버지가 주신 장구 덕분에 부자가 된 것입니다. 막내도 다시 갈림길로 돌아와 집을 짓고 살았습니다.

❖ ❖ ❖

After a while, a goblin started to sniff. "I can smell a human! I can smell a human!" he said.

Then the other goblins started to sniff, saying, "The human smell is coming from the ceiling."

They then tried to climb up to the ceiling.

"Oh, I'm so dead! If I had a sword then I could kill them," the second son thought. And then he spun his millstone. The sound of the millstone's spinning was quite loud, because he spun the empty millstone hard.

Hearing the sound, the goblins threw away their bats and ran away. Goblins are usually quite timid, so they had thought that the sound coming from the millstone was the sound of the house falling down. When the second son came down from the ceiling, he found many goblin bats. Because of his father's millstone, he was now rich. He brought the goblin bats back to the crossroads, built a house and lived there.

The youngest son walked and walked with the *jang-gu* drum, down the right road. It became night, and he was still in the mountains, but he could find no house. Wandering from place to place, he came upon some tigers who tried to eat him. He climbed up a tree, but the tigers stood on each other's shoulders in order to reach him.

"Oh, I am dead. If I had a sword then I could kill them," the youngest son thought. And then he played his *jang-gu* drum. He even sang a song while he did so. This made the tigers excited, and they started to dance while still standing on each other's shoulders. As they danced, they shrugged their shoulders, swung their front legs, and crouched on their back legs. This caused them to fall and collapse in a heap, breaking their necks and killing them.

When the youngest son came down from the tree, he saw many dead tigers. He skinned them and sold their valuable furs. Because of his father's *jang-gu* drum he was now rich. He also went back to the crossroads, built a house and lived there.

❖ ❖ ❖

Pre-Reading Questions (answer in Korean or English)

a. 당신은 자식들에게 어떤 것을 유산으로 주고 싶습니까?

b. 제목이 주는 이 이야기에 대한 단서는 무엇입니까?

c. 이 이야기에서 중요한 물건이나 등장인물을 추측할 수 있습니까?

Vocabulary

세 가지 **se gaji** three kinds of

유산 **yusan** legacy

삼형제 **samhyeongje** the three brothers

담뱃대 **dambaesdae** a pipe

맷돌 **maesdol** a millstone

장구 **jang-gu** a double-headed drum

장례식 **janglyesig** a funeral

나이가 많다 **naiga manhda** to be older

힘이 세다 **him-i seda** to be strong

(장구를) 잘 치다 **jal chida** to be good at playing

걷다 **geodda** to walk

세 갈래 **se gallae** to be three-forked

헤어지다 **heeojida** to part

돈을 벌다 **don-eul beolda** to earn money

돌아오다 **dol-aoda** to come back

짓다 **jisda** to build

왼쪽 **oenjjog** left

가운데 **gaunde** middle

오른쪽 **oleunjjog** right

밤새 **bamsae** all night

냄새 **naemsae** a smell

맡다 **matda** to smell

갈림길 **gallimgil** a crossroad

목말을 타다 **mogmal-eul tada** to stand on one's shoulders

신이 나다 **sin-i nada** to become excited

어깨 **eokkae** a shoulder

무너지다 **muneojida** to collapse

Culture Notes

A **jang-gu** is a traditional drum with two heads covered in animal skin. Since its distinctive characteristic is its hourglass shape, at one point it was called a **saeyogo**, which means a drum with a narrow waist. It has been frequently used in various styles of Korean traditional music from **Nongak** (commoners' music), to **Talchum** (a masked dance), to aristocratic ritual events.

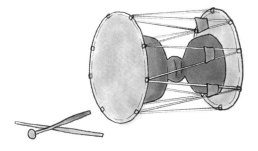

Comprehension Questions

a. 첫째가 갈림길로 돌아오기 전에, 어떤 일이 일어났습니까?

b. 둘째가 갈림길로 돌아오기 전에, 어떤 일이 일어났습니까?

c. 막내가 갈림길로 돌아오기 전에, 어떤 일이 일어났습니까?

Writing Activity

등장인물들 사이의 관계를 보여 주는 이야기 지도를 만드십시오.

Create a story map that shows the connections between the characters.

도깨비가 준 보물

Dokkaebiga Jun Bomul

옛날 옛날에 한 남자가 살았습니다. 남자는 정말 착하고 친절한 사람이었지만, 콩과 보리를 구별하지 못하고, 1 더하기 2 가 무엇인지 모르는 조금 모자라는 사람이었습니다. 그래서 남자의 부모님은 아주 걱정이 많았습니다. 어느 날 밤, 남자의 부모님은 남자에 대해서 이야기를 했습니다.

"우리가 죽고 나면 저 아이가 어떻게 살지 걱정이에요."

"나도 그래요. 우리가 죽기 전에 세상 구경이나 하고 오게 합시다. 그렇게 하면 괜찮을지도 몰라요."

이렇게 이야기한 후 남자의 부모님은 남자를 집에서 내보냈습니다. 남자는 가방 하나만 가지고 집을 나왔습니다.

걷다가 걷다가 남자가 아직 산 속에 있는데 밤이 되었습니다. 근처에 빈 집이 하나 있어서 남자는 그 집에서 자고 가게 되었습니다. 그런데 그 집은 도깨비의 집이었습니다. 무섭게 생긴 도깨비가 집에서 나와서, "잘됐다. 나하고 1 년만 살자." 라고 말했습니다. 남자는 무서워서 그러기로 했습니다. 1 년이 지나고, 도깨비가 보자기를 하나 주었습니다.

"이 보자기를 펴 놓고 박수를 한 번 치면 쌀이 생긴다."

도깨비가 말했습니다. 그래서 남자가 보자기를 펴 놓고 박수를 한 번 쳤더니 하얀 쌀이 많이 생겼습니다. 남자는 그 보자기를 가지고 집으로 출발했습니다.

집에 가는 길에 다시 밤이 되었습니다. 그래서 한 집에서 자고 가게 되었습니다. 남자는 집 주인에게 보자기를 맡기면서 말했습니다.

"절대로 이 보자기를 펴 놓고 박수를 치면 안 돼요."

주인은 왜 박수를 치면 안 되는지 궁금했습니다. 그래서 남자 몰래 보자기를 펴 놓고 박수를 쳤습니다. 그랬더니 또 쌀이 많이 생겼습니다. 주인은 남자의 보자기가 가지고 싶어서 그 보자기를 숨겨 놓고 다음날 다른 보자기를 주었습니다.

남자는 그것도 모르고 집에 돌아가서 부모님께 자랑을 했습니다.

"어머니 아버지, 제가 쌀이 생기는 보자기를 가져왔어요."

The Treasure Given by a Goblin

❖ *This story is about a fool and three gifts from a goblin.* ❖

Once upon a time, there was a man. The man was very nice and kind, but he was a fool who could not distinguish the difference between a bean and barley corn, and did not know the sum of one plus two. Therefore, his parents worried about him very much. One night, his parents talked about him.

"I am worried about how he could possibly live alone after we die," said his mother.

"Me too! Let's make him go out and see the world before we die. It might be helpful if he did so," said his father.

After talking, his parents sent him out to see the world. The man left the house with only a bag.

As he walked and walked, it became night, and he was still in the mountains. There was an empty house nearby, so the man decided to stay there. However, this was a goblin's house.

A scary-looking goblin came out of the house and said, "Oh, good! Come live with me for a year."

The man decided to do so because he was scared. After one year, the goblin gave him a wrapping cloth.

"If you spread out this wrapping cloth and clap once, rice will come out of it," the goblin said.

The man then spread out the wrapping cloth, clapped once, and a lot of white rice came out of it. The man then started on his way home with the wrapping cloth.

On his way home, it became night again, so once again he stayed at a house.

He gave the wrapping cloth to the owner of the house and said, "You should never spread out this wrapping cloth and clap."

This made the owner of the house curious, so he spread out the wrapping cloth and clapped when the man was not looking. When he did that, a lot of rice came out. The owner of the house then wanted to keep the man's wrapping cloth, so he hid it and gave the man a different one the next day.

Without knowing that the wrapping cloth had been changed, the man went back home and showed it off to his parents.

남자가 보자기를 펴 놓고 박수를 쳤지만, 아무것도 나오지 않았습니다. 부모님은 한숨을 쉬면서 남자를 야단쳤습니다.

"1 년 동안 세상 구경을 하고도 아직 아무것도 모르면 어떡하니. 다시 나가서 더 배우고 와라."

남자는 다시 가방 하나만 가지고 집을 나왔습니다.

걷고 걷다가 다시 도깨비의 집으로 가게 되었습니다. 도깨비가 집에서 나와서, "보자기를 잃어버렸다고? 그럼 나하고 1 년만 더 살자." 라고 말했습니다. 남자는 도깨비와 1 년을 더 살았습니다. 1 년이 지나고, 도깨비가 말을 한 마리 주었습니다.

"이 말의 엉덩이를 때리면 금이 나온다."

도깨비가 말했습니다. 그래서 남자가 말의 엉덩이를 때렸더니 금이 많이 나왔습니다. 남자는 그 말을 데리고 집으로 출발했습니다.

집에 가는 길에 다시 밤이 되었습니다. 그래서 한 집에서 자고 가게 되었습니다. 남자는 집 주인에게 말을 맡기면서 말했습니다.

"절대로 이 말의 엉덩이를 때리면 안 돼요."

주인은 왜 엉덩이를 때리면 안 되는지 궁금했습니다. 그래서 남자 몰래 말의 엉덩이를 때렸습니다. 그랬더니 또 금이 많이 나왔습니다. 주인은 남자의 말이 가지고 싶어서 그 말을 숨겨 놓고 다음날 다른 말을 주었습니다.

남자는 그것도 모르고 집에 돌아가서 부모님께 자랑을 했습니다.

"Mother and father, I brought this wrapping cloth that makes rice come out."

The man spread out the wrapping cloth and clapped, but nothing came out of it.

His parents scolded him with a sigh: "How did you learn nothing while you were out seeing the world for a year? Go out again and learn some more."

The man left the house once again with only his bag.

He walked and walked, and came to the goblin's house again.

The goblin came out and said, "Did you lose the wrapping cloth? Then let's live together for one more year."

The man lived with the goblin for another year. After one year, the goblin gave the man a horse.

"If you hit this horse's backside, gold will come out," the goblin said.

The man hit the horse's backside, and gold came out. He then started on his way home with the horse. On his way home, it became night once again, so he stayed at the same house as before.

The man entrusted the horse to the owner of the house, saying, "You should never hit this horse's backside."

This made the owner of the house curious, so he hit the horse's backside when the man was not looking, and a lot of gold came out. He wanted to keep the horse, so he hid the horse and gave the man a different horse the next day.

Without knowing the horse had been changed, the man returned home and showed it off to his parents.

"어머니 아버지, 제가 금이 나오는 말을 데려왔어요."

남자가 말의 엉덩이를 때렸지만, 똥 말고는 아무것도 나오지 않았습니다. 부모님은 한숨을 쉬면서 남자를 야단쳤습니다.

"2 년 동안 세상 구경을 하고도 아직 아무것도 모르면 어떡하니. 다시 나가서 더 배우고 와라."

남자는 다시 가방 하나만 가지고 집을 나왔습니다.

걷고 걷다가 다시 도깨비의 집으로 가게 되었습니다. 도깨비가 집에서 나와서, "말을 잃어버렸다고? 그럼 나하고 1 년만 더 살자." 라고 말했습니다. 남자는 도깨비와 1 년을 더 살았습니다. 1 년이 지나고, 도깨비가 방망이를 한 개 주었습니다.

"이 방망이한테 '때려라' 라고 하면 방망이가 사람을 때린다."

도깨비가 말했습니다. 남자는 그 방망이를 가지고 집으로 출발했습니다.

집에 가는 길에 다시 밤이 되었습니다. 그래서 한 집에서 자고 가게 되었습니다. 남자는 집 주인에게 방망이를 맡기면서 말했습니다.

"절대로 이 방망이한테 '때려라' 라고 하면 안 돼요."

주인은 보자기와 말처럼 이번에도 좋은 것이 나올 것이라고 생각했습니다. 그래서 남자 몰래 방망이한테 '때려라'라고 했습니다. 그랬더니 방망이가 주인을 마구 때리기 시작했습니다. 주인이 아파서 도망치면 쫓아와서 때리고, 다시 도망치면 다시 쫓아와서 때렸습니다. 주인이 남자가 자는 방으로 도망쳐서 엉엉 울며 말했습니다.

"아이고, 내가 잘못했습니다. 저번에 훔친 보자기와 말을 돌려주겠습니다. 제발 살려 주세요."

그래서 남자는 도깨비가 준 보자기와 말을 다시 찾았습니다. 보자기와 말을 가지고 집에 가니 부모님이 반가워했습니다. 남자와 부모님은 쌀이 나오는 보자기와 금이 나오는 말을 가지고 행복하게 살았습니다.

❖ ❖ ❖

"Mother and father, I brought a horse that gold comes out of."

The man hit the horse's backside, but nothing that came out except poop.

His parents scolded him again, sighing: "How did you learn nothing while you were out seeing the world for two years? Go out again and learn more."

The man left home again with only one bag.

He walked and walked, and came to the goblin's house again.

The goblin came out house and said, "Did you lose the horse? Then let's live together for one more year."

The man lived with the goblin for one more year.

After one year, the goblin gave him a bat. "If you say 'hit' to this bat, this bat will hit someone," the goblin said.

The man started on his way home with the bat.

On his way home, it became night once again, so he decided to stay at the same house as before.

The man entrusted the bat to the owner of the house and said, "You should never say 'Hit!' to this bat."

The owner of the house thought good things would come out of the bat, just like the wrapping cloth and the horse, so he said "Hit!" to the bat when the man was not looking. The bat then started severely beating the owner of the house. The owner of the house took off running away because he was being beaten, but the bat chased after him and continued to hit him.

He ran to the room where the man was sleeping, and said loudly while crying, "Oh, I did wrong! I'll return the wrapping cloth and the horse I stole from you. Please save me!"

Thus, the man got back the wrapping cloth and the horse that the goblin had given him. His parents were glad to see him when he returned home with both the wrapping cloth that produced rice and the horse that produced gold, and they all lived happily ever after.

❖ ❖ ❖

Pre-Reading Questions (answer in Korean or English)

a. 당신은 도깨비에게서 선물을 받고 싶습니까?

b. 이 이야기에서 도깨비의 중요한 성격을 추측할 수 있습니까?

c. 이 이야기에서 도깨비가 어떤 보물을 줄 것인지 추측할 수 있습니까?

Vocabulary

보물 **bomul** a treasure

콩 **kong** a bean

보리 **boli** a barley

더하기 **deohagi** plus

조금 **jogeum** a little bit

모자라다 **mojalada** to be a fool

세상 구경 **sesang gugyeong** sightseeing the world

가방 **gabang** a bag

빈 집 **bin jib** an empty house

보자기 **bojagi** a wrapping cloth

그것도 모르고 **geugeosdo moleugo** without knowing it

자랑을 하다 **jalang-eul hada** to show off

한숨을 쉬다 **hansum-eul swida** to sigh

야단치다 **yadanchida** to scold

아무것도 모르다 **amugeosdo moleuda** to know nothing

엉덩이 **eongdeong-i** one's backside

금 **geum** the gold

똥 **ttong** poop

출발하다 **chulbalhada** to start on one's way

절대로 **jeoldaelo** never

안 되다 **an doeda** should not do

그래서 **geulaeseo** therefore, thus

그랬더니 **geulaessdeoni** then

마구 **magu** severely

잘못하다 **jalmoshada** to do wrong

저번에 **jeobeon-e** last time

제발 **jebal** please

Culture Notes

In Korean traditional fairytales, goblins sometimes carried baseball-type bats. A goblin's bat can make money or food, or whatever its owner wants it to make. In this story, a good person receives a goblin's bat as a present, and a bad person who is greedy gets beaten by it.

Comprehension Questions

a. 왜 남자의 부모님은 남자에게 세상 구경을 시키려고 했습니까?
b. 도깨비가 준 보물들은 무엇이었습니까?
c. 남자가 보물을 집에 가져갔을 때 왜 아무것도 나오지 않았습니까?

Writing Activity

이 이야기의 등장인물 한 명을 인터뷰 할 질문을 쓰세요. 반 친구들 중 한 명을 그 등장인물로 생각하고, 그 친구를 인터뷰하세요.

Write interview questions for one character in the story. Interview one of your class-mates who will respond as that character.

소원을 들어주는 그림

Sowon-eul Deul-eojuneun Geulim

옛날 옛날에 두 친구가 살았습니다. 두 사람은 어렸을 때부터 아주 친한 친구였습니다. 콩 하나가 있어도 둘이 나누어 먹을 만큼 친했습니다. 그래서 두 친구는 서로 약속을 했습니다.

"나중에 커서 내가 잘 되면 너를 도와 주고, 네가 잘 되면 나를 도와 줘서 같이 잘 살자." 두 친구가 모두 잘 커서 결혼을 했습니다. 하지만 결혼하면서 서로 멀리 헤어지게 되었습니다. 한 친구는 시골에 살고, 다른 한 친구는 서울에 살았습니다. 그리고 시간이 많이 지나자, 시골에 사는 친구가 아주 가난해졌습니다. 과거 시험을 보아도 자꾸 떨어지고, 돈은 자꾸 없어지고, 먹을 것도 없어서 가족이 모두 굶어야 했습니다. 그래서 시골 친구가 자기 아내에게 말했습니다.

"내가 어렸을 때 나를 도와 주기로 한 친구가 있습니다. 이 친구를 찾아가야겠어요." 하지만 서울까지 여행을 떠날 돈이 없었습니다. 그래서 아내가 머리를 잘라 팔아서 돈을 주었습니다. 시골 친구는 그 돈을 가지고 서울 친구를 찾아가기로 했습니다.

시골 친구가 서울로 가 보니 서울 친구의 집이 아주 컸습니다. 하인도 여러 명 있었습니다. 시골 친구가 문을 두드리니 서울 친구가 아주 반가워했습니다. 반갑게 인사를 하고 나서 시골 친구가 말했습니다.

"네가 잘 사는 것을 보니 정말 반갑다. 하지만 나는 어떻게 이렇게 불행한지 먹고 살 음식도 없어. 그래서 아내의 머리를 자른 돈으로 여기까지 왔다."

그러자 서울 친구가 말했습니다.

"진작 오지 왜 이제야 왔어? 걱정하지 말고 우리 집에서 며칠 있다가."

서울 친구는 시골 친구를 잘 대접해 주었습니다.

며칠 후, 시골 친구가 말했습니다.

"고맙다. 하지만 이제 가 봐야겠어. 내가 음식을 살 돈을 좀 빌려 줄 수 있겠니?"

그러자 서울 친구는 돈을 주지 않고 그림을 한 장 주었습니다. 황새

A Painting That Will
Make Your Wishes Come True

❖   *This story is about two friends and mysterious paintings.*   ❖

Once upon a time, there were two friends. The two had been very close ever since they were kids. They were so close that if they only had one bean between them, they would split it and eat it together. The two friends made a promise to each other saying, "Someday, when we're older, if I'm doing well I will help you and if you're doing well you will help me, so we'll both live well."

The two friends grew up and got married. After they married, they lived at a distance from each other. One friend lived in the country, while the other lived in Seoul. A lot of time went by, and the friend who lived in the country became very poor. In the past, he had often failed exams and often lost money, so he did not have anything to eat, and his family was constantly hungry.

He said to his wife, "When I was young, I had a friend who said he would help me. I'm going to go find him."

Since he did not have the funds to travel to Seoul, his wife cut off her hair and sold it, giving him the money. He took the money and left for Seoul. Arriving in Seoul, he found his friend living in a large house. His friend even had several servants. When he knocked on the door, his friend was very happy to see him.

After greeting each other excitedly, the country friend said, "I'm glad to see that you're living so well. But I am unhappy without having even enough food to eat. My wife even had to cut her hair so I could get the money to come here."

When he said this, his friend responded, "Why didn't you come sooner? Don't worry. Rest at my home for a couple days before you leave."

The city friend was a gracious host to his country friend.

After a couple of days the country friend said, "Thank you. But I need to be going. Will it be possible for me to borrow money for food?"

After he said this, his city friend did not give him any money, but instead gave him a painting—a painting of a single crane.

The country friend became angry, saying, "When we were young we said we would help each other out. How can you be like this? What use is this painting?"

His friend responded, "This painting will help you. Whenever there is a dif-

가 한 마리 그려져 있는 그림이었습니다. 시골 친구는 화가 났습니다.

"우리가 어렸을 때 서로 도와 주기로 했는데 어떻게 이럴 수 있어? 이 그림으로 무엇을 하라는 거야?"

그러자 서울 친구가 말했습니다.

"이 그림이 너를 도와 줄 거야. 힘들 때마다 회초리로 황새의 다리를 한 번씩 때려. 그럼 좋은 일이 생길 거야."

시골 친구는 서울 친구의 말을 이해하지 못했지만, 서울 친구를 믿기로 했습니다. 그래서 그 그림을 가지고 다시 집으로 출발했습니다. 서울 친구가 시골 친구의 뒤에서 말했습니다.

"아무리 힘들어도 하루에 한 번씩만 황새 다리를 때려야 해. 하루에 꼭 한번이야." 시골 친구는 알았다고 했습니다.

집으로 돌아가는 길에, 시골 친구는 황새의 다리를 때리면 어떤 일이 일어날지 아주 궁금해졌습니다. 그래서 그림을 꺼내서 황새 다리를 한 번 때려 보았습니다. 그랬더니, 그림에서 돈이 나왔습니다. 시골 친구는 그 돈을 가지고 집에 가지 않고 놀러다녔습니다. 돈을 다 쓰면 다시 그림을 꺼내서 황새의 다리를 때렸습니다. 그러면 또 돈이 나왔습니다. 며칠을 그렇게 놀러 다니다가 시골 친구가 생각했습니다.

"하루에 한 번으로는 부족해. 황새 다리를 많이 때려서 돈을 많이 받아야겠다."

그래서 시골 친구는 그림을 펴 놓고 황새 다리를 자꾸 때렸습니다. 때릴 때마다 돈이나왔습니다. 그렇게 한 스무 번 때리자 황새 다리가 부러졌습니다. 그리고 돈도 나오지 않았습니다. 시골 친구는 나온 돈을 다 쓰고는 다시 서울 친구에게 갔습니다.

"내가 황새 다리를 자꾸 때려서 다리가 부러졌다. 어떻게 하지?"

시골 친구가 말했습니다.

"내가 그럴 줄 알았다."

서울 친구가 말했습니다. 서울 친구는 또 시골 친구를 잘 대접해 주었습니다.

시골 친구가 다시 집에 가려고 할 때, 서울 친구가 이번에는 항아리가 그려진 그림을 주었습니다.

"이 그림이 너를 도와 줄 거야. 힘들 때마다 항아리를 똑똑 두드려. 그럼 좋은 일이 생길 거야. 이번에는 꼭 하루에 한 번씩만 두드려야 해.

ficult time, hit the crane's legs with a cane, one by one. Do this, and good things will happen."

The country friend did not understand what his Seoul friend was saying, but decided to believe him. So, he took the painting and left for home.

His city friend said to him as he left, "No matter how hard it is you must, everyday, one by one, smack the crane's legs. Everyday, exactly once!"

The country friend promised to do so.

On the road to his house, the country friend wondered what would happen if he smacked the crane's legs. So, pulling out the painting, he tried hitting the crane's legs just once. Having done this, money began flowing out of the painting. The country friend took this money, but went out on the town instead of returning home. Having spent all the money, once again, he pulled up the painting and hit the crane's legs. Once again, money came out.

After several days of this, the country friend thought, "Doing this once a day isn't enough. I'll have to hit the crane's legs many times to get lots of money."

So, the country friend got out the painting and repeatedly hit the crane's legs. Every time he hit it, money came out. After about twenty times of hitting it like this, the crane's legs broke and money stopped flowing out.

Using all the money he had left, he once again went to his friend in Seoul, saying, "The crane's legs broke because I hit them repeatedly. What do we do now?"

His city friend answered, "I knew this would happen."

He once again received and graciously hosted his country friend.

When his country friend was about to leave once again, his friend gave him a painting of a pot and said, "The painting will help you. Whenever there is a difficult time, knock on the pot. If you do this, good things will happen. This time, exactly one time only must you knock. Each day, exactly once."

The country friend said, "Okay."

As he was on the road back home, the country friend wondered what would happen if he knocked on the pot. So, pulling the painting out, he knocked on the pot once. As he did this, money came out of the painting. The country friend took this money and once again, did not return home but went out on the town. After using up all the money, he would pull out the painting and knock on the pot, and more money would flow out.

하루에 꼭 한 번씩이야."

시골 친구는 알았다고 했습니다.

집으로 돌아가는 길에, 시골 친구는 항아리를 두드리면 어떤 일이 일어날지 아주 궁금해졌습니다. 그래서 그림을 꺼내서 항아리를 한 번 두드려 보았습니다. 그랬더니, 그림에서 돈이 나왔습니다. 시골 친구는 그 돈을 가지고 또 집에 가지 않고 놀러다녔습니다. 돈을 다 쓰면 다시 그림을 꺼내서 항아리를 두드렸습니다. 그러면 또 돈이 나왔습니다. 며칠을 그렇게 놀러 다니다가 시골 친구가 생각했습니다.

"하루에 한 번으로는 부족해. 항아리를 많이 두드려서 돈을 많이 받아야겠다."

그래서 시골 친구는 그림을 펴 놓고 항아리를 자꾸 두드렸습니다. 두드릴 때마다 돈이 나왔습니다. 그렇게 한 스무 번 때리자 항아리가 깨졌습니다. 그리고 돈도 나오지 않았습니다. 시골 친구는 나온 돈을 다 쓰고는 다시 서울 친구에게 갔습니다.

"내가 항아리를 자꾸 두드려서 항아리가 깨졌다. 어떻게 하지?"

시골 친구가 말했습니다.

"내가 그럴 줄 알았다."

서울 친구가 말했습니다. 서울 친구는 또 시골 친구를 잘 대접해 주었습니다.

시골 친구가 다시 집에 가려고 할 때, 서울 친구가 이번에는 상자가 그려진 그림을 주었습니다.

"이 그림이 너를 도와 줄 거야. 힘들 때마다 상자에 손을 넣어. 그럼 좋은 일이 생길 거야. 이번에는 꼭 하루에 한 번씩만 손을 넣어야 해. 하루에 꼭 한 번씩이야. 안 그러면 우리 둘 다 죽어."

After playing around for a couple of days, the country friend thought, "Once a day isn't enough. If I knock on the pot more, I'll get more money."

So, he pulled out the painting and repeatedly knocked on the pot. Every time he knocked, money came out. He continued like this for twenty times, until the pot broke, and no more money came out. He used the money to return to his friend in Seoul.

The country friend said, "I repeatedly knocked on the jar and it broke. What do we do now?"

His city friend answered, "I knew this would happen."

He once again received and graciously hosted his country friend.

When the country friend was about to leave again, this time his friend gave him a painting of a box and said, "This painting will help you. Whenever there is a difficult time, lay your hand on the box. If you do this, good things will happen. This time, you must only lay your hand on the box once. Each day, exactly once. If you don't do this, we will both die."

The country friend promised.

As he was on the road returning to his house, the country friend wondered what would happen if he placed his hand on the box. So, pulling out the painting, he laid his hand on the box one time. As he did this, money came out of the painting. He again took this money and went out on the town. After using up all the money, he would pull out the painting and lay his hand on the box. Doing this, more money would come out.

After a couple days of playing around, he thought, "Once a day isn't enough. I need to get more money from the box." So, he pulled out the painting and repeatedly placed his hand on the box. Every time he placed his hand on the box,

시골 친구는 알았다고 했습니다.

집으로 돌아가는 길에, 시골 친구는 상자에 손을 넣으면 어떤 일이 일어날지 아주 궁금해졌습니다. 그래서 그림을 꺼내서 상자에 손을 한 번넣어 보았습니다. 그랬더니, 그림에서 돈이 나왔습니다. 시골 친구는 그돈을 가지고 또 집에 가지 않고 놀러다녔습니다. 돈을 다 쓰면 다시 그림을 꺼내서 상자에 손을 넣었습니다. 그러면 또 돈이 나왔습니다. 며칠을그렇게 놀러 다니다가 시골 친구가 생각했습니다.

"하루에 한 번으로는 부족해. 상자에서 돈을 많이 꺼내야겠다."

그래서 시골 친구는 그림을 펴 놓고 상자에 자꾸 손을 넣었습니다. 손을 넣을 때마다 돈이 나왔습니다. 이번에는 스무 번, 서른 번, 마흔 번이 지나도 상자가 깨지지 않았습니다. 그래서 시골 친구는 자꾸 자꾸 돈을 꺼냈습니다.

그 때, 왕궁의 큰 창고에서 돈이 없어지고 있었습니다. 창고 지키는 사람이 보니까 돈 꾸러미가 창고의 굴뚝에서 날아가고 있었습니다. 그래서창고 지키는 사람들이 날아가는 돈을 따라가 보자, 시골 친구가 그림에서 돈을 자꾸 꺼내고 있었습니다. 그래서 창고 지키는 사람들이 시골 친구를 왕궁으로 잡아왔습니다. 어디서 그 그림을 받았냐고 물으며 시골친구를 때리자, 시골 친구가 이제까지 있었던 일을 모두 말했습니다. 그래서 서울 친구도 왕궁으로 잡혀왔습니다.

"너희들은 왕궁의 돈을 훔쳐서 살려 줄 수 없다."

왕이 말했습니다. 서울 친구 말대로 이제 둘 다 죽게 되었습니다.

사형 날짜가 되어서 시골 친구와 서울 친구가 둘 다 끌려 나왔습니다.서울 친구가 왕에게 빌었습니다.

"죽기 전에 그림을 한 번만 그리게 해 주세요."

왕은 그러라고 했습니다. 서울 친구는 큰 종이에 말 한 마리와 채찍을하나 그렸습니다. 그리고 시골 친구를 데리고 그림 속의 말에 올라탔습니다. 서울 친구가 "가자!" 하고 채찍으로 말을 한 번 때리자 말이 살아서 하늘로 날아올랐습니다. 왕은 시골 친구와 서울 친구를 잡을 수 없었고, 그 다음에 어떻게 되었는지는 아무도 모릅니다.

❖ ❖ ❖

money came out. This time, twenty, thirty, forty times passed, and the box did not break. So, he continued on many, many times to keep getting money.

At the same time, money from the palace's large warehouse began disappearing. The warehouse guards saw piles of money flying out of the warehouse chimney. The money flew out each time the country friend got money out of the painting. The guards followed the money, found the country friend, and grabbed him. As they beat him, they asked where he got the painting from. The country friend told them everything. They therefore brought both friends to the palace.

The king said, "You both have stolen the palace's money so we can't let you live."

Just as the Seoul friend had warned, both of them would die.

On the day of their execution, the two friends were dragged forward.

The friend from Seoul said to the king, "Before I die, please allow me to paint one painting."

The king allowed him to do so.

The Seoul friend drew one horse and one whip on a piece of paper. He led his country friend onto the painting, and then got on the horse saying, "Let's go!" He grabbed the whip, hitting the horse once, and the horse came to life and flew toward the sky. The king was unable to catch the two friends, and no one knows what happened to them thereafter.

❖ ❖ ❖

Pre-Reading Questions (answer in Korean or English)

a. 이것은 실제 이야기처럼 보입니까? 아니면 가상의 이야기처럼 보입니까? 왜 그렇게 생각합니까?

b. 제목이 주는 이 이야기에 대한 단서는 무엇입니까?

c. 만약 당신에게 소원을 들어 주는 그림이 있다면 어떤 소원을 빌고 싶습니까?

Vocabulary

소원 **sowon** a wish

들어 주다 **deul-eo juda** to grant a wish

나누다 **nanuda** to split/share

서로 **seolo** each other

시골 **sigol** the countryside

서울 **seoul** Seoul

굶다 **gulmda** not able to eat anything

여행하다 **yeohaenghada** to travel

불행하다 **bulhaenghada** to be unhappy

진작 **jinjag** already/sooner

그림 **geulim** a painting

황새 **hwangsae** a crane

하루 **halu** one day (time period)

다리 **dali** a leg

부러지다 **buleojida** to be broken

항아리 **hang-ali** a pot

두드리다 **dudeulida** to knock

상자 **sangja** a box

스무 번 **seumu beon** twenty times

서른 번 **seoleun beon** thirty times

마흔 번 **maheun beon** forty times

왕궁 **wang-gung** the palace

창고 **chang-go** a warehouse

잡아오다 **jab-aoda** to catch and bring a person

잡혀오다 **jabhyeooda** to be caught and brought

사형 날짜 **sahyeong naljja** the day of execution

채찍 **chaejjig** a whip

Culture Notes

A well-done painting can make nature and animals seem alive. In the Silla Dynasty there was a man named Solgeo who drew very well. He drew a pine tree on a temple's wall so well that it looked real, and birds flew into the wall thinking it was a real tree.

Comprehension Questions

a. 왜 시골 친구는 서울 친구를 찾아가려고 했습니까?

b. 서울 친구가 시골 친구에게 준 그림들은 어떤 그림들이었습니까?

c. 어떻게 마지막에 두 친구가 도망칠 수 있었습니까?

Writing Activity

이 이야기의 사건들을 순서대로 표시하세요. 화이트보드에 포스트잇을 사용해서 사건의 순서를 표시하십시오. 다른 학생들이 표시한 순서와 일치합니까?

Create a timeline that shows the events in the story. Use Post-it notes on the whiteboard to show the timeline. Does your timeline match others'?

가짜 명궁

Gajja Myeong-gung

옛날 옛날에 한 시골 총각이 있었습니다. 이 시골 총각은 나이가 서른이 넘었는데 결혼도 못 하고 힘들게 일만 했습니다. 그러다 보니 너무 재미가 없다는 생각이 들었습니다. 그래서 논밭을 팔아 돈을 받아 가지고 무작정 서울로 올라갔습니다.

시골 총각은 서울에서 장사를 하려고 했습니다. 그런데 서울 사람들이 이 시골 총각이 장사를 하려고 물건을 사면 돈을 비싸게 받았습니다. 시골 총각이 너무 착하고 어리숙해 보였기 때문입니다. 그래서 시골 총각은 가지고 온 돈을 다 잃어버렸습니다. 그렇게 서너 달이 지났습니다.

그런데 이 시골 총각이 그 동안 서울을 여기저기 돌아다니면서 한 가지 배운 게 있습니다. 그게 뭐냐면, 서울 사람들은 사람의 겉모습을 보고 대접한다는 겁니다. 아무것도 없는 건달이라도 아래위로 잘 차려 입고 활을 메고 다니면 좋은 대접을 받고, 아무리 좋은 사람이라도 낡은 옷을 입고 돌아다니면 어딜 가나 푸대접을 받는 것입니다. 그래서 시골 총각은 생각했습니다.

'에이, 나는 여기에서 돈을 벌 수 없을 것 같으니 사람들에게 좋은 대접이나 많이 받고 미련 없이 집으로 돌아가자.'

그래서 시골 총각이 얼마 남지 않은 돈으로 새 옷을 사 입고 활을 사서 메고 서울을 돌아다녔습니다. 그랬더니 과연 사람들이 시골 사람을 다르게 보기 시작했습니다. 그러니 시골 총각은 저절로 어깨도 으쓱해지고 괜히 걸음걸이에도 힘이 들어갔습니다. 그렇게 돌아다니다가 시골 총각이 죽은 꿩 두 마리를 길에서 주웠습니다. 꿩을 줍기는 주웠는데 어디 넣을 데가 없어서 화살에 두 마리를 꿰어 가지고 갔습니다. 또 다시 길을 가다가 밥을 먹으러 식당에 들어갔습니다. 그런데 식당 주인이 화살에 꿰인 꿩을 보고는 호들갑을 떨었습니다.

"아이고, 이 분이 화살 하나로 꿩을 두 마리나 잡으셨다."

그 소리를 듣고 식당에 있던 사람들이 우르르 몰려들어 구경을 하며 떠들었습니다.

A Fake Expert Archer

❖ *This story is about a man who pretended to be a good archer.* ❖

Once upon a time, there was a countryside bachelor. This countryside bachelor was in his thirties, and having been unable to marry he did nothing but work. Realizing his situation, an unpleasant thought entered his head. He sold his fields, took the money, and moved to Seoul without any thought or preparation. He intended to do business in Seoul, but because he looked kind and naïve, people sold things to him at expensive prices. After three or four months like this, he had lost all his money.

"Well since we probably will not be able to earn money here, let's get a lot of good hospitality from the people (here) and then return home without regret."

During his time of wandering around Seoul, the countryside bachelor had learned one important thing. If you were to ask what he learned, it was that people from Seoul treat a person according to how they look. Even if you have nothing—and are a good-for-nothing—if you dress like you are a member of the upper class and carry a bow, you will be treated well. Likewise, however good a person you may be, if you wear outdated clothes as you go about, you will receive unkind treatment no matter where you go.

Therefore, the countryside bachelor took his little remaining money and purchased new clothes and a bow. He put them on and began walking around Seoul. After he did this, sure enough, people began seeing him differently, and he naturally found himself raising his shoulders in pride and strengthening his step. As he wandered around like this, he found two dead pheasants in the street. Picking them up, he found he did not have anywhere to set them, so he shoved them on an arrow and continued on his way. Then, on the same road, he went into a restaurant.

The restaurant owners saw the two pheasants pierced with one arrow and made a big fuss about it, saying, "Wow! This man killed two pheasants with one arrow!"

The restaurant patrons heard this and swarmed around him, murmuring as they tried to get a look, "He must be an expert archer. This is the first time I've ever seen two pheasants killed with one arrow."

People began clapping in admiration of him. The countryside bachelor never said that he had killed the pheasants with one arrow. He was too embarrassed

"명궁이네, 명궁이야. 화살 하나로 꿩을 두 마리나 잡은 걸 보기는 처음이야."

사람들이 모두 손뼉을 치며 감탄했습니다. 시골 총각은 아니라고 설명하기가 부끄럽고 귀찮아서 그냥 아무 말도 하지 않고 가만히 있었습니다. 그랬더니 그중에 한 사람이 시골 총각을 따로 불러서 말했습니다.

"나는 정승 댁 손님인데, 드릴 말씀이 있으니 저와 같이 갑시다."

그래서 시골 총각은 그 사람을 따라 정승네 집으로 갔습니다. 그 사람은 고래등 같은 기와집으로 들어가더니 시골 총각을 정승 앞에 데리고 가서 소개했습니다.

"정승님, 이 사람이 아주 명궁이라 여기 데리고 왔습니다."

정승이 아주 기뻐하며 시골 총각 말고는 다 방에서 나가라고 했습니다. 모두가 방에서 나간 다음 정승이 시골 총각에게 말했습니다.

"며칠 전부터 우리 집에 이상한 일이 생겨서 명궁을 찾고 있었다. 어떤 일이냐면, 뒷마당 감나무에 밤만 되면 부엉이 한 마리가 와서 울고 가는데, 그 부엉이가 울고 나면 사람이 죽는다. 벌써 아들 셋을 잃고 딸 하나 남았는데, 또 부엉이가 와서 우는 날이면 하나 남은 딸마저 죽을까봐 무섭다. 그 동안 명궁이란 명궁은 다 불러서 부탁했지만, 아무도 부엉이를 쏘아 죽이지 못했다. 오늘 밤 우리 집에서 자고, 부엉이를 쏘아 죽여 줘. 그러면 이 은혜는 잊지 않겠다."

시골 총각에게는 너무 어려운 일이었습니다. 시골 총각은 활을 어떻게 쓰는지도 모르는데, 어떻게 명궁들이 잡지 못한 부엉이를 잡을까요? 하지만 여기까지 와서 못 하겠다고 말할 수도 없었습니다. 그래서 시골 총각은 에라 모르겠다 하고 큰소리를 쳤습니다.

"걱정 마세요. 제가 오늘 밤에 꼭 그 부엉이의 눈을 쏘아 죽이겠습니다."

하지만 밤이 가까워지니까 시골 총각은 눈앞이 캄캄했습니다. 그런데 하늘이 무너져도 솟아날 구멍은 있다고, 이렇게 저렇게 생각하다 보니 좋은 방법이 떠올랐습니다. 시골 총각은 저녁이 되기를 기다렸다가, 옷을 다 벗고 맨살을 새까맣게 칠한 다음 부엉이가 날아온다는 감나무 위로 올라갔습니다. 시골 총각은 다 올라가서 감나무 나뭇가지에 딱 붙어서 매달려 있었습니다. 온몸에 먹물을 칠해 놔서 캄캄한 밤에는 시골 총각이 잘 보이지 않았습니다. 그대로 밤이 깊어지고, 부엉이 한 마리가

and annoyed to explain anything, so he simply stood there quietly and did not say a word.

In the middle of this, one person called out, saying, "I'm a guest at the minister's house. He has something to say to you, come with me."

So, the bachelor followed the man to the minister's house. The man brought him to an enormous, tiled room.

Once they were in front of the minister, he introduced the countryside bachelor: "Mr. Minister, this man is an expert archer, so I have brought him here."

The minister was very happy and told everyone else to leave the room.

After everyone had left the room, the minister said to the countryside bachelor, "Since a few days ago, a strange thing has been happening in our house, and we have been looking for an expert archer. At night, an owl will hoot in the persimmon tree in the back yard, and then leave. After the owl hoots, someone will die. I've already lost three sons, and only have one daughter remaining. I'm fearful that if the owl comes yet again to hoot, my daughter will die. I've called several expert archers, but none have been able to shoot and kill the owl. Stay at our house tonight to shoot and kill the owl. If you do so, I won't forget this kindness."

This was a very difficult task that was set before the countryside bachelor. He did not even know how to use a bow. How was he supposed to shoot an owl that other expert archers could not hit?

Having come this far, however, he could not refuse, so he said to himself, "What the heck?" and began to talk through his hat to the minister: "Don't worry. Tonight I will shoot the owl between the eyes and kill it."

As night came closer, the countryside bachelor grew hopeless in the light of what had to be done. However, where there is life, there is hope, and so after thinking this way and that, a plan emerged. As he waited, he removed his clothes, covered his naked body in black ink, and climbed to the top of the persimmon tree. Having climbed to the top of the tree, he chose a branch and, sticking to it closely, hung from the tree. His whole body now painted with ink, the countryside bachelor could barely be seen in the pitch-black night. The night deepened and when the owl arrived, the bachelor happened to be seated on a branch just above it. He quickly grabbed the owl by its neck and wrung it, killing the owl. He took the dead owl and stuck an arrow into its left eye, and then threw it into the yard. After this he cleaned up, put on his clothes, and went back inside to sleep.

날아오더니시골 총각의 바로 위에 있는 나뭇가지에 앉았습니다. 시골 총각이 얼른 손으로 부엉이 모가지를 잡아서 단번에 비틀어 죽였습니다. 그리고 죽은 부엉이의 왼쪽 눈에 화살을 꽂아서 마당에 던져 놨습니다. 그리고 나서 시골 총각은 몸을 씻고 옷을 입고 들어와서 잠을 잤습니다.

다음날 아침에 정승이 마당에 나가 보니 부엉이가 왼쪽 눈에 화살을 맞고 죽어 있었습니다. 정승이 감탄했습니다.

"정말 백년에 하나 나올까 말까한 명궁이군."

정승이 아주 좋아하면서 시골 총각을 자기 딸과 결혼하게 했습니다. 시골 총각 덕분에 이 딸이 목숨을 건졌다고 생각했기 때문입니다. 가난했던 시골 총각은 순식간에 부자가 되었습니다. 정승 딸과 결혼해서 정승의 집 이웃집에 살면서 예쁜 부인과 참 재미있게 잘 살았습니다.

그런데 큰일이 났습니다. 나라에서 활쏘기 대회가 열린 것입니다. 온 나라에서 명궁들이 활쏘기 대회에 참석하기 위해 모였습니다. 시골 총각은 이미 명궁이라고 여기저기 소문이 나서 나가지 않을 수가 없었습니다. 시골 총각은 한숨을 쉬며 어쩔 수 없이 활쏘기 대회에 나갔습니다.

대회에 나가 보니 다른 사람들은 모두 활을 너무 잘 쏘았습니다. 아주 멀리에서 과녁을 겨냥하고 활을 쏘는데도 활을 쏠 때마다 과녁의 정중앙에 화살이 박혔습니다. 시골 총각은 사실 활을 어떻게 들고 어디를 겨냥해야 하는지도 몰랐습니다.

모두들 활을 다 쏘고 드디어 시골 총각 차례가 됐습니다. 시골 총각은 활을 가지고 나가기는 했지만 활을 어떻게 쏘아야 하는지 몰라서 그냥 남들을 따라서 활시위만 잔뜩 당기고 가만히 서 있었습니다. 구경하는 사람들이 모두 숨을 죽이고 보고 있는데, 시골 총각은 아무리 기다려도 활시위를 놓지 않았습니다. 한참 그러고 있다가 정승이 답답해서 시골 총각에게 달려갔습니다.

"어서 활을 쏘지 않고 뭐 해?"

정승이 시골 총각을 재촉하면서 활시위를 당기고 있는 팔을 툭 건드렸습니다. 그 바람에 화살이 과녁 쪽이 아니라 하늘로 날아갔습니다. 그런데 마침 그 때 꿩 두 마리가 날아가고 있었습니다. 화살이 그 중 한 마리의 왼눈을 딱 맞혀서 떨어뜨렸습니다. 구경하던 사람들이 모두 감탄을 했지만 시골 총각은 정승에게 화를 냈습니다.

The next morning the minister went into the yard and saw the dead owl with an arrow in its left eye.

Awestruck, he said, "This truly is an expert archer, the likes of which are only to be seen once in a hundred years."

The minister really liked the countryside bachelor. He gave his daughter to him in marriage, because he thought that his daughter was still alive, thanks to the archer's skill. The once-poor countryside bachelor became rich in a single moment.

Having married the minister's daughter, he began living next door with his beautiful wife. But then a bigger problem emerged—a nationwide archer's tournament opened—expert archers gathered from all over the country to participate in it. Since the talk of the town was that he was an expert archer, there was no way he could avoid taking part, so taking a deep breath he went to the tournament.

When he arrived, he discovered that everyone shot extremely well. Arrows were shot from great distances aimed at the centers of the targets, and every arrow was a bull's eye. However, in all truthfulness, he did not even know how to raise a bow or take aim. After everyone else had shot their arrows, finally, it was his turn. He took a bow and went forward, but as he did not know how to use it. Imitating the other archers, he drew back the bowstring clumsily, and stood

"에이, 장인 어른 때문에 망쳤습니다. 두 마리를 화살 하나로 한꺼번에 맞히려고 했는데 팔을 건드리는 바람에 한 마리밖에 못 맞혔잖아요. 저는 이제 다시는 활을 쏘지 않겠습니다."

시골 총각은 그리고 나서 정말로 다시는 활을 쏘지 않았습니다. 그리고 행복하게 잘 살았습니다.

❖ ❖ ❖

Pre-Reading Questions (answer in Korean or English)
a. 활을 쏴 본 적이 있습니까?
b. 이 이야기에서 중요한 등장인물을 추측할 수 있습니까?
c. 이 이야기에서 어떤 일이 일어날까요?

Vocabulary

서른 **seoleun** thirty (years of age)
넘다 **neomda** to be over, past
논 **non** a rice paddy
밭 **bat** a field of grain
무작정 **mujagjeong** thoughtlessly
장사 **jangsa** a business
어리숙하다 **eolisughada** to be naïve
겉모습 **geotmoseub** an appearance, a look
좋은 대접 **joh-eun daejeob** a good treatment
푸대접 **pudaejeob** a poor treatment
꿩 **kkwong** a pheasant
명궁 **myeong-gung** an expert archer
정승 **jeongseung** the government minister
부엉이 **bueong-i** an owl

큰소리를 치다 **keunsolileul chida** to talk through his hat
눈앞이 캄캄하다 **nun-ap-i kamkam-hada** to be hopeless (idiom)
단번에 **danbeon-e** only once
비틀다 **biteulda** to wring
순식간에 **sunsiggan-e** quickly
대회 **daehoe** a tournament
과녁 **gwanyeog** a target
정중앙 **jeongjung-ang** the center
활시위를 당기다 **hwalsiwileul danggida** to draw back the bowstring
재촉하다 **jaechoghada** to rush
마침 **machim** just in time
감탄하다 **gamtanhada** to amaze/admire at
망치다 **mangchida** to mess up/spoil

there silently. Everyone held their breath and watched, but no matter how long they waited, he did not release the bowstring.

Having waited a good while, the minister, feeling stifled, rushed to him and said, "What're you doing by not quickly shooting the arrow?"

As the minister pushed against him, his hand holding back the bowstring snapped down. The arrow did not fly toward the target, but was instead carried by the wind into the sky. At that moment, two pheasants were flying by. The arrow hit one of the birds in the left eye, and it dropped to the ground.

The onlookers were amazed, but the archer got angry with the minister and said, "Hey! I messed up because of you! I was trying to hit two with one arrow, but was only able to hit one because my arm dropped down. Now I will never shoot a bow again."

The fake expert archer never did shoot a bow again, and lived happily ever after.

✤ ✤ ✤

Culture Notes

Archery is a martial art that has been a part of the Korean culture for a long time. Archeologists speculate that the bow has been used in Korea ever since the Stone Age. In the old days, the Chinese people had a term for people in the east who were good at archery: **Dongyi**. Even today, Koreans receive some of the highest scores in archery at the Olympics.

Comprehension Questions

a. 왜 사람들은 시골 총각이 명궁이라고 생각했습니까?

b. 시골 총각이 오기 전에 정승에게 어떤 일이 일어났습니까?

c. 활쏘기 대회에서 왜 시골 총각은 정승에게 화를 냈습니까? 그는 정말로 화가 났습니까?

Writing Activity

이 이야기의 등장인물 한 명에게 질문할 인터뷰질문을 쓰세요. 반 친구들 중 한 명을 그 등장인물로 생각하고, 그 친구를 인터뷰하세요.

Write interview questions for one character in the story. Interview one of your classmates who will respond as that character.

시어머니 길들이기

Sieomeoni Gildeul-igi

옛날 옛날에 아주 성격이 나쁜 시어머니가 있었습니다. 얼마나 성격이 나쁘냐면, 그 시어머니가 며느리를 괴롭히지 않으면 남들이 이상하게 생각할 만큼 성격이 나빴습니다. 심지어 아무 이유도 없이 며느리를 괴롭혔습니다. 빨리 걸으면 빨리 걷는다고, 느리게 걸으면 느리게 걷는다고 화를 내고, 밥을 할 때 밥을 많이 하면 이 밥을 누가 다 먹냐고, 밥을 조금 하면 이 밥으로 어떻게 온 식구가 다 먹냐고 화를 냈습니다.

그래서 이 집에 아들은 딱 한 명인데 벌써 며느리가 세 번이나 바뀌었습니다. 첫번째 며느리는 시어머니 앞에서 방귀 뀌었다고 친정에 보내고, 두 번째 며느리는 밥상을 나르다가 엎질렀다고 친정에 보내고, 세 번째 며느리는 화를 낼 일이 없으니까 말버릇이 나쁘다고 친정에 보내 버렸습니다. 이렇게 며느리를 셋씩이나 쫓아내고 나니까, 아들이 정말 잘생기고 집도 부자인데도 아무도 이 집 아들과 결혼하려고 하지 않았습니다. 그런데 이 동네에 사는 한 처녀가 그 집 아들과 결혼하고 싶다고 했습니다. 처녀의 부모님은 그 집 시어머니 소문을 듣고 처녀를 말렸습니다.

"그 집에 시집가서 세 달을 넘긴 며느리가 없다. 그런데도 그 남자와 결혼하고 싶니? 잘생기고 돈 많은 게 다가 아니야."

처녀는 부모님의 말을 듣더니 생글생글 웃으며 말했습니다.

"저한테도 다 생각이 있어요. 걱정 마세요."

처녀의 부모님은 걱정이 많이 되었지만 처녀를 믿고 그 남자와 결혼을 시켰습니다. 시어머니는 세 번째 며느리를 쫓아내고 나서는 며느리를 괴롭히지 못해서 마침 심심했는데, 새 며느리가 들어오니 기다렸다는 듯이 괴롭히기 시작했습니다. 그래도 새 며느리는 얼굴색 한번 바꾸지 않고 시어머니의 말을 잘 따랐습니다. 어처구니 없는 일로 혼을 내도 "예, 잘못했습니다." 라고 하면서 시어머니가 때리면 맞고 혼내면 혼났습니다. 시아버지는 그런 며느리를 보기가 힘들었습니다.

"애야, 너희 시어머니가 너무 힘들게 하지 않니? 그냥 친정으로 돌아가는 게 어때?"

The Taming of the Mother-in-Law

❖ *This story is about a mean mother-in-law and a wise daughter-in-law.* ❖

Once upon a time there was a very bad mother-in-law. To show the measure of how bad her personality was, if the mother-in-law did not torment her daughter-in-law for even one day, others thought, "She's behaving strangely today." She harassed her daughter-in-law for no reason at all. If her daughter-in-law was walking fast, then the mother-in-law became angry that she walked fast. If her daughter-in-law was walking slowly, then the mother-in-law became angry that she walked slowly. If her daughter-in-law cooked a lot of rice, then the mother-in-law would say, "Who could eat all of this rice?" But if her daughter-in-law cooked just enough rice, then the mother-in-law would comment, "How can all the family members get full on such a small amount of rice?"

Thus, even though the house had only one son, over time it has seen three different daughters-in-law. The first daughter-in-law was sent home to her family because she farted in front of her mother-in-law. The second daughter-in-law was sent home to her family because she overturned the table while carrying it. Since there was nothing to get angry about with the third daughter-in-law, she sent her back to her family with the pretext that she had a foul mouth. After having driven out this last daughter-in-law, there was no one who wanted to marry her son, even though he was very handsome, and the household was rich.

Despite this history, one unmarried woman in the town decided to marry the son. Naturally, her parents tried to stop her: "No one who's married into this family has stayed more than three months. Do you still want to marry the man? Even though the man is handsome and rich, that's not everything."

The woman listened to her parents and answered with a smile, "I have an idea. Don't worry."

Though her parents were very worried about her, they trusted her and let her marry the man. By this time, the man's mother was bored because she had had no daughter-in-law to torment, after having sent the third daughter-in-law away. So, when the new daughter-in-law arrived, it was just what she had been waiting for.

However, the new daughter-in-law always did exactly as her mother-in-law told her to do, without any change of countenance. Even when her mother-

시아버지가 걱정하며 말했습니다. 며느리는 생글생글 웃으며 대답했습니다.

"어머님께서 제가 무엇을 잘못했는지 알려 주시는 겁니다. 저는 괜찮습니다."

새 며느리가 이렇게 말한 것이 소문이 나서 온 동네 사람들이 저렇게 얌전하고 착한 며느리는 또 없을 거라고 칭찬을 했습니다.

그러다가 어느 날, 시아버지와 남편이 밖으로 나갔습니다. 집에는 새 며느리와 시어머니밖에 없었습니다. 그러자 새 며느리가 밧줄과 회초리를 들고 시어머니한테 갔습니다. 시어머니는 깜짝 놀라 물었습니다.

"이 못된 것아, 그것들은 왜 들고 왔어?"

"예, 어머님 버릇을 고쳐 드리려고요."

새 며느리가 얼굴색 한번 바꾸지 않고 생글생글 웃으며 시어머니를 밧줄로 기둥에 꽁꽁 묶었습니다. 그러고는 회초리 든 손에 침을 탁 뱉었습니다. 시어머니는 갑자기 생각도 못한 일을 당해서 말도 한 마디 못하고 묶여 있었습니다.

"어머님이 미워서 이러는 게 아니라 버릇을 고쳐 드리려고 이러는 것입니다. 저를 미워하지 마세요."

새 며느리가 말했습니다. 그러더니 회초리로 시어머니를 사정 없이 때렸습니다. 시어머니는 어이없고 분하고 원통해서 아무 말도 하지 못했습니다. 새 며느리는 한참 그렇게 시어머니를 때리고 나서 다시 생글생글 웃으며 말했습니다.

"오늘은 여기까지 하겠습니다. 하지만 어머님이 버릇을 못 고치시면 또 때릴 수밖에 없어요."

새 며느리는 시어머니를 기둥에서 풀어 주고 시어머니가 화내기 전에 잽싸게 숨었습니다. 시어머니는 화는 나는데 화를 낼 곳이 없어서 맨발로 문 밖에 나가 동네 사람들이 들으라고 고래고래 소리를 질렀습니다.

"아이고, 동네 사람들. 내 말 좀 들어 보세요. 우리 집 새 며느리가 날 회초리로 때렸어요."

하지만 동네 사람들은 아무도 시어머니의 말을 믿지 않았습니다. 시어머니는 며느리를 괴롭히기로 유명하고, 새 며느리는 얌전하고 착하기로 유명했기 때문입니다. 그래서 모두들 저 시어머니가 또 며느리를 괴롭히다가 완전히 미쳐 버린 것 같다고 수군거렸습니다. 이렇게 동네 사

in-law scolded her over something ridiculous, she would just say, "Yes, I was wrong." And, when her mother-in-law hit her, she accepted it, just like she accepted the scolding.

Her father-in-law found this all difficult to watch. "Sweetheart, doesn't your mother-in-law make your life too difficult? Why don't you just go back to your parents?" said the father-in-law worriedly.

The daughter-in-law answered, smiling, "It was only my dear mother telling me what I did wrong. I am okay."

This conversation occurred out in the open where everyone could hear. The whole village praised her, saying that there could be no other daughter-in-law who was as decent and kind as her.

Then one day, her husband and father-in-law went out, leaving only her and her mother-in-law at home. She went to her mother-in-law holding a rope and a cane.

Surprised, the mother-in-law asked, "You bad girl, why did you bring those?"

"Why, to correct your bad habits."

She tied her mother-in-law tightly to a pole using the rope, without changing countenance. Then she spat on the hand holding the cane. The mother-in-law had allowed herself to be tied up without saying a word, because it was all so unexpected.

"This is not because I hate you, but because I am trying to correct your habits. Please do not hate me," she said. She then beat her mother-in-law severely with the cane. Dumbfounded, vexed, and resentful, the mother-in-law was rendered speechless.

The new daughter-in-law beat her mother-in-law for a long time, and then said with a smile, "That's it for today. But if you don't correct your habits, I'll have no choice but to beat you again."

She released her mother-in-law from the pole, and quickly ran away before her mother-in-law could lash out in anger.

The mother-in-law was furious, but there was no one to release her anger on, so she went outside in her bare feet and shouted loudly so that all the people in the village could hear, "Oh, neighbors! Listen to me! My new daughter-in-law beat me with a cane!"

However, no one in the village believed her words, because she was famous for tormenting her daughters-in-law, and her new daughter-in-law was well-

람들이 아무도 자기 말을 믿지 않으니까 시어머니는 더 화가 나서 남편을 찾아가 대성통곡을 했습니다.

"아이고, 영감. 며느리가 날 회초리로 때렸어요. 아이고, 아파."

하지만 시아버지도 시어머니의 말을 믿지 않았습니다.

"쯧쯧, 저 할멈이 이제는 완전히 미쳐 버렸군. 새 며느리가 당신을 때리다니, 그걸 말이라고 해?"

그러자 시어머니가 이번에는 아들을 찾아가 대성통곡을 했습니다.

"애야, 네 부인이 회초리로 날 때렸단다."

아들도 그 말을 믿지 않았습니다.

"아이고, 어머니. 거짓말을 하려면 좀 그럴듯한 거짓말을 하세요."

시어머니는 어이없고 분하고 원통해서 속이 새까맣게 탔습니다. 저녁이 돼서 시아버지와 남편이 돌아오니까 새 며느리는 언제 시어머니를 때렸냐는 듯이 얌전해져서, 시어머니가 욕을 해도 "예, 잘못했습니다." 라고 하면서 시어머니가 때리면 맞고 혼내면 혼났습니다. 그럴수록 시어머니는 더 화가 났습니다.

known as decent and kind. Instead, everyone whispered that the mother-in-law had gone completely crazy while tormenting her daughter-in-law.

Since no one in the village believed her, she became even more furious, going to her husband and wailing loudly, "Oh, dear! My daughter-in-law beat me with a cane! Oh, it hurts!"

However, he did not believe her either. "Tsk! Tsk! That old woman is now completely crazy. Your new daughter hit you? Is that really what you are saying?"

Then, she went to her son and wailed loudly, "Sweetheart, your wife beat me with a cane!"

Her son did not believe her words either. "Oh, mom. If you want to lie, say something plausible."

Because she was dumbfounded, vexed, and resentful, the mother-in-law ate herself up inside. When the father-in-law and the husband came back home that night, the new daughter-in-law acted as kind as usual, as if she had not hit her mother-in-law. And, even when her mother-in-law said bad things to her, she just answered, "Yes, I was wrong." And when her mother-in-law hit her, she allowed it, just as she accepted her scoldings. This made the mother-in-law even more furious still.

다음날, 시아버지와 남편이 일하러 나가자마자 새 며느리는 또 시어머니를 밧줄로 기둥에 꽁꽁 묶어 놓고 회초리로 때렸습니다.

"어머님이 아직도 버릇을 못 고치셨으니 또 때릴 수밖에 없습니다."

그 날도 시어머니는 며느리한테 회초리로 실컷 맞고 온 동네에 떠들고 다녔지만 아무도 시어머니의 말을 믿지 않았습니다.

그 다음날, 시아버지와 남편이 일하러 나가자마자 새 며느리가 또 밧줄과 회초리를 들고 시어머니한테 갔습니다. 그랬더니 시어머니가 펑펑 울면서 새 며느리에게 말했습니다. "내가 잘못했다, 내가 잘못했어. 이제 다시는 그러지 않을 테니까 이제 그만해라." 그러자 새 며느리도 시어머니를 때린 것을 울면서 사과하고, 그 다음부터는 시어머니에게 효도하면서 서로 사이좋고 행복하게 살았습니다.

❖ ❖ ❖

Pre-Reading Questions (answer in Korean or English)
a. 어떤 사건이 설명되거나 묘사될 것이라고 생각합니까?
b. 이 이야기에서 중요한 등장인물을 추측할 수 있습니까?
c. 만약 당신의 시어머니가 당신을 괴롭힌다면, 당신은 어떻게 할 것입니까?

Vocabulary
시어머니 **sieomeoni** a mother-in-law
길들이기 **gildeul-igi** the taming
괴롭히다 **goelobhida** to harass
빠르다 **ppaleuda** to be fast
느리다 **neulida** to be slow
며느리 **myeoneuli** a daughter-in-law
엎지르다 **eopjileuda** to spill
말버릇이 나쁘다 **malbeoleus-i nappeuda** to have a foul mouth
기다렸다는 듯이 **gidalyeossdaneun deus-i** like one was waiting for
얼굴색 한번 바꾸지 않고 **eolgulsaeg hanbeon bakkuji anhgo** without changing countenance
시아버지 **siabeoji** a father-in-law
보기가 힘들다 **bogiga himdeulda** too difficult to see

친정 **chinjeong** a married woman's parents' home
소문이 나다 **somun-i nada** to be in the air
회초리 **hoecholi** a cane
버릇을 고치다 **beoleus-eul gochida** to correct one's bad habit
사정없이 **sajeong-eobs-i** severely
어이가 없다 **eoiga eobsda** to be dumbfounded
미치다 **michida** to be crazy
대성통곡 **daeseongtong-gog** to wail
그럴듯하다 **geuleoldeushada** to be plausible
속이 새까맣게 타다 **sog-i saekkamahge tada** to eat oneself up
실컷 **silkeos** as much as one likes

The next day, as soon as her father-in-law and husband went to work, she tied her mother-in-law tightly to a pole with a rope, and beat her with the cane again.

"Because you haven't yet corrected your habits, there is no choice but to beat you again."

Once again, her mother-in-law was beaten with a cane by her daughter-in-law, and talked about this news to the whole village, but no one believed her words.

The next day, right after her father-in-law and husband went to work, she came to the mother-in-law again, holding the rope and cane.

At this point, her mother-in-law burst into tears, and said, "I did wrong, I did wrong. I won't do it again, so stop."

Then her new daughter-in-law cried and apologized for beating her. From then on, she observed her filial duties to her mother-in-law, and the whole family lived happily ever after.

❖ ❖ ❖

떠들고 다니다 **tteodeulgo danida** to talk about it everywhere
잘못하다 **jalmoshada** to do wrong
사과하다 **sagwahada** to apologize
효도하다 **hyodohada** to do one's filial duty

Culture Notes
In the old days, it was not acceptable for a daughter-in-law to defy her mother-in-law. In fact, in other Korean traditional fairytales the daughter-in-law either submits meekly to or gets bullied by her mother-in-law. This story is very surprising because a daughter-in-law not only defies her mother-in-law, but resorts to violence to solve a problem.

Comprehension Questions
a. 새 며느리는 시어머니에게 무엇을 했습니까?
b. 왜 마을 사람들은 시어머니의 말을 믿지 않았습니까?
c. 시어머니가 옛날 며느리들을 친정에 보낸 이유는 무엇이었습니까?

Writing Activity
이 이야기 속 한 등장인물의 성별을 바꾸고, 이야기의 부분을 다시 써서 성별이 다르면 그 등장인물이 어떻게 다르게 행동할지 보여 주세요.
Choose one character in the story and change his/her gender. Then rewrite sections of the story to show how that character might act differently if he/she were a different gender.

임금님 귀는 당나귀 귀

Imgeumnim Gwineun Dangnagwi Gwi

옛날 옛날에 한 임금님이 있었습니다. 이 임금님은 남에게 말하지 못하는 걱정이 하나 있었습니다. 갑자기 어느 날부터 임금님의 귀가 쑥쑥 자라더니 이제는 당나귀 귀만큼 커진 것입니다. 사흘 동안 자고 일어나면 이만큼, 또 자고 일어나면 또 이만큼씩 커져서 그렇게 되었습니다. 그러고 나서 귀가 더 자라지는 않았지만, 거울을 보면 귀가 너무 컸습니다. 사람인지 당나귀인지 모를 정도였습니다.

귀가 커져서 불편하기도 했지만, 임금님의 걱정은 귀가 이렇게 커진 것을 사람들이 알게 되는 것이었습니다. 임금님이기 때문에 사람들에게 존경받아야 하는데, 귀가 이렇게 당나귀처럼 크면 존경받는 게 아니라 다들 임금님의 귀를 비웃을 것 같았습니다. 그래서 임금님은 밖에 나가지 못했습니다. 다른 사람들에게는 몸이 아프다는 핑계를 대고 방에 틀어박혀서 아무도 임금님의 방에 들어오지 못하게 했습니다. 하지만 평생 그러고 살 수는 없어서, 임금님이 이 생각 저 생각을 하다가 모자를 만드는 사람을 임금님의 방으로 불렀습니다.

그래서 아주 솜씨 좋기로 유명한 모자 장수가 불려 왔습니다. 모자 장수가 임금님의 방에 들어가 임금님의 귀를 보니, 당나귀 귀보다 더 큰 것 같았습니다. 모자 장수는 자꾸 웃음이 나왔지만 임금님 앞이라 웃을 수가 없었습니다. 그래서 입을 꼭 다물고 임금님 앞에 엎드렸습니다.

"임금님, 왜 저를 부르셨습니까?" 모자 장수가 말했습니다.

"가능한 빨리 큰 모자를 만들어 줘라. 얼마나 커야 하냐면, 내 귀가 감쪽같이 덮일 만큼 커야 한다. 그리고 내 귀가 이렇다는 것을 누구에게도 말하지 말아라. 누군가 내 귀에 대해 알게 된다면, 내 귀가 이렇다는 걸 아는 사람은 나말고 너밖에 없으니까, 너를 잡아서 목을 자를 것이다."

그래서 모자 장수는 아주아주 큰 모자를 만들어서 임금님에게 바쳤습니다. 임금님이 그 모자를 써 보니 모자가 자기 머리보다 더 큰 것 같았지만, 그래도 귀는 보이지 않았습니다. 그래서 임금님은 병이 다 나았다고 하고 방 밖으로 나왔습니다. 사람들이 임금님을 보았지만 다들 모자가 크다는 이야기만 하고, 그 큰 모자 속에 당나귀 귀가 있는 것은 몰랐습니다.

176

The King Has Donkey's Ears

❖ *This story is about a king's ears and the mysterious happening related to them.* ❖

Once upon a time, there was a king. This king had a bad problem, but he could not tell anyone about it. Suddenly one day, the king's ears began growing, becoming as big as donkey's ears. Every morning for three days straight, when he woke up he discovered that his ears had become bigger. When he went to sleep again and woke up, his ears were bigger still. For the sake of this tale, that is about the size of it, because his ears did not grow anymore after that. However, whenever he looked in the mirror, he could see that his ears were too big, so big that he was afraid nobody would know whether he was a person or a donkey.

He felt uncomfortable because his ears had grown, but his biggest worry was that people became aware of it. He thought that he should be esteemed by the people because he was king. However, if his ears were this big—as big as a donkey's—he would not be respected. Everyone would likely laugh at his ears, so he did not go outside. He stayed inside a room with the excuse that he was sick, and prevented anyone from entering, but he could not live like this for the rest of his life, so he had to think of something.

He called a man who made hats into his room. This hatter was very famous for his skill. When the hatter came into the king's room and saw the king's ears, to him they seemed bigger than donkey's ears. He wanted to laugh, but could not do so because he was in front of the king, so he shut his mouth tightly and fell down prostrate.

"Why did you call me, King?" the hatter asked.

"Make a big hat as soon as possible. It should be big enough to cover my ears entirely. And do not tell anyone that my ears are like this. If someone finds out about my ears, I will catch you and cut your throat, because you are the only one who knows that my ears are like this, except for me."

So, the hatter made a very big hat and gave it to the king. When the king wore the hat, it seemed bigger than his head, but you could not see his ears, so the king said that he was no longer sick and left his room. People saw the king wearing his hat, but they did not know that it hid donkey's ears underneath it. They talked about the hat because it was very big.

그런데 모자 장수는 모자를 임금님에게 바치고 나서부터 미친 사람처럼 하고 다녔습니다. 모자 장수는 임금님의 당나귀 귀를 보기는 봤는데, 그 웃긴 이야기를 아무에게도 하지 못했습니다. 그게 답답해서 모자 장수는 혼자 아무 일 없이 허허 웃고 다녔습니다. 밥 먹다가도 허허, 길 가다가도 허허, 잠 자다가도 허허, 당나귀 귀 생각만 하면 웃음이 나오기 때문이었습니다. 모자 장수를 아는 사람이 그 모습을 보고 물었습니다.

"무슨 좋은 일이 있어서 그렇게 허허 웃고 다녀?"

모자 장수는 또 허허 웃으며 대답했습니다.

"아무 것도 아니야. 그럴 일이 있어. 허허, 허허."

다들 모자장수가 미쳤다며 혀를 찼습니다.

날이 갈수록 모자 장수는 정말로 미쳐 버릴 것 같았습니다. 누구에게든 임금님의 당나귀 귀 이야기를 하고 싶어서 입이 근질근질한 걸 억지로 참았더니 너무 힘들었습니다. 정말 길을 가다가 아무나 붙잡고 임금님 귀는 당나귀 귀라고 말하고 싶었지만, 그러면 임금님이 자기를 죽일 것 같았습니다. 하고 싶은 말을 너무 참으면 병이 난다는 말이 있는데, 이 모자 장수가 정말로 병이 났습니다.

모자 장수는 병이 나서 방 안에만 누워 있었습니다. 누워서 계속 생각해 보니, 말을 하지 않아서 이렇게 아파서 죽으나 말을 하고 임금님에게 죽으나 똑같으니까 차라리 말을 하고 죽는 것이 나은 것 같았습니다. 그래서 어느 날 밤에 모자 장수는 집 근처에 있는 대나무 숲으로 갔습니다. 다른 사람들에게 말하면 임금님이 그 말을 들은 다른 사람들도 죽일까봐 걱정이 되었기 때문입니다. 그래서 모자 장수는 아무도 없는 대나무 숲에 가서 크게 소리를 질렀습니다.

"임금님 귀는 당나귀 귀다!"

"임금님 귀는 당나귀 귀다!"

대나무 숲에 대고 크게 소리를 지르고 나니 십 년 묵은 체증이 한꺼번에 다 내려가는 것 같고, 앓던 이가 쑥 빠지는 것 같았습니다. 모자 장수는 그렇게 소리를 지르고 나서 아주 편안하게 죽었습니다.

그런데 이 모자 장수가 죽고 난 다음부터 이상한 일이 생겼습니다. 매일 밤 대나무숲에 바람이 불면 이상한 소리가 나는 것입니다. 바람이 불면 대나무 잎이 바람에 흔들리면서 사람 말소리가 들렸습니다.

"스스스 스스스, 임금님 귀는 당나귀 귀다!"

However, the hatter began behaving as a crazy man after he gave the hat to the king. He had seen the king's donkey ears, but he could not tell the funny story to anyone. That made him feel stifled, so he laughed to himself at times for no reason. He laughed while eating, he laughed while walking on the road, and he laughed while sleeping, because it made him laugh when he just thought about the donkey's ears.

Someone who knew the hatter asked him to share what was going on: "What makes you laugh like that?"

The hatter answered, laughing even more. "It's nothing. There's nothing to share. Haha! Haha!"

Everyone began clicking their tongues, saying that the hatter was crazy.

As the days went by, the hatter thought he would go crazy. It was so hard to hold his tongue when he was bursting with news he was dying to share about the king. He could not talk to anyone, but he really wanted to grab someone along the street and tell him that the king's ears were donkey's ears. However, the king had promised to kill him. There is a saying that if you hold in too much even though you have a lot of things to say, you will become ill. Well, this hatter got really ill.

The hatter just lay in his room because he was so ill. But as he was lying down, he thought and thought and decided that he'd rather died (by the king's order) for talking about the king's ears—since he would still die because of his illness. Either way, he would die. Therefore, one night, the hatter went to the bamboo forest near his house. He went there because he worried that if he told his story to other people, the king would kill them.

So, the hatter went to a lonely bamboo forest, and shouted loudly, "The king's ears are donkey's ears! The king's ears are donkey's ears!"

After shouting loudly in the bamboo forest, it seemed as though a huge weight had been lifted off his chest. He felt quite relieved, and was able to die in peace.

However, something strange happened after the hatter died. Every night, when the wind blew, the bamboo leaves were shaken by the wind and a voice was heard: "Swish! Swish! The king's ears are donkey's ears! Swish! Swish! The king's ears are donkey's ears!"

Since people had heard the sound from the bamboo forest, they began talking about the king's ears. This rumor reached the king, who got angrier and

"스스스 스스스, 임금님 귀는 당나귀 귀다!"

사람들이 대나무 숲에서 나는 소리를 듣고 임금님의 귀 이야기를 하니까, 임금님도 그 소문을 듣게 되었습니다. 임금님은 크게 화를 내면서, 그 대나무숲의 대나무를 다 베어 버리라고 명령했습니다. 임금님의 신하들이 대나무를 다 베어 버리자 이상한 소리는 들리지 않았습니다. 하지만, 그 다음 해에 다시 대나무가 자라자 또 바람이 불 때마다 이상한 소리가 들렸습니다. 그래서 임금님은 대나무를 다 뽑아 버리고 그 자리에 동백나무를 심으라고 명령했습니다. 하지만 그 동백나무도 밤이 되고 바람이 불면 동백나무 잎이 바람에 흔들리면서 사람 말소리가 들렸습니다.

"싸그락 싸그락, 임금님 귀는 당나귀 귀다!"

"싸그락 싸그락, 임금님 귀는 당나귀 귀다!"

사람들이 동백나무 숲에서 나는 소리를 듣고 또 임금님의 귀 이야기를 하니까, 임금님이 이번에는 동백나무도 모두 뽑아 버리라고 명령했습니다. 그랬더니 그 다음부터는 아무 소리도 들리지 않았습니다. 하지만 이미 소문이 퍼져서, 이제는 임금님 귀가 당나귀 귀인 것을 모르는 사람은 아무도 없었습니다.

angrier. He finally ordered that the entire bamboo forest be cut down. When the king's servants cut down all the bamboo trees, no strange sound was heard. However, after the bamboo trees grew again the next year, a strange sound was heard again when the wind blew. Therefore, the king ordered that the bamboo trees be rooted up, and camellias planted in their place. However, when it became night and the wind blew through the camellia leaves, a voice was heard again when the leaves shook: "Rustle! Rustle! The king's ears are donkey's ears! Rustle! Rustle! The king's ears are donkey's ears!"

People heard the sound from the camellia grove, and began talking about the king's ears again, so the king ordered that all the camellia trees be rooted up. After that, no sound was heard from the grove. However, the rumor had already spread, until there was no one who did not know that the king's ears were donkey's ears.

❖ ❖ ❖

Pre-Reading Questions (answer in Korean or English)

a. 당나귀 귀를 본 적이 있습니까?

b. 어떤 사건이 설명되거나 묘사될 것이라고 생각합니까?

c. 당신의 귀에 대해 걱정해 본 적이 있습니까?

Vocabulary

임금님 **imgeumnim** a king (honorific form)

걱정 **geogjeong** a worry

귀 **gwi** an ear

쑥쑥 자라다 **ssugssug jalada** to become bigger

당나귀 **dangnagwi** a donkey

사흘 **saheul** three days

이만큼 **imankeum** this much

거울 **geoul** a mirror

존경받다 **jongyeongbadda** to be honored

핑계 **ping-gye** an excuse

평생 **pyeongsaeng** for the rest of one's life

모자 장수 **moja jangsu** a hatter

엎드리다 **eopdeulida** to lie face down

가능한 빨리 **ganeunghan ppalli** as soon as possible

감쪽같다 **gamjjoggatda** to be just as it was

바치다 **bachida** to dedicate

날이 갈수록 **nal-i galsulog** as days go by

입이 근질근질하다 **ib-i geunjilgeunjilhada** to be full of news

똑같다 **ttoggatda** to be the same

차라리 **chalali** rather than

대나무 **daenamu** a bamboo tree

십 년 묵은 체증이 내려가다 **sib nyeon mug-eun chejeung-i naelyeogada** a huge weight has been lifted off one's chest

한꺼번에 **hankkeobeon-e** at once

앓던 이가 빠지는 것같다 **alhdeon iga ppajineun geos gatda** to feel sudden relief

명령하다 **myeonglyeonghada** to order

동백나무 **dongbaegnamu** a camellia tree

뽑아 버리다 **ppob-a beolida** to root up

Culture Notes

Korean kings wore crowns to show their dignity. The golden crown from the Silla Dynasty is especially famous, as it is not only a big crown covered in elaborate gold decorations, but it is also covered in gems. Scholars today question if this crown was ever actually worn, because it is quite heavy. They think that the kings could not have worn this crown every day, but must have worn it only when there was an important event, in order to show his dignity.

Comprehension Questions

a. 왕은 왜 모자 장수를 불렀습니까?
b. 모자 장수는 왕을 위해 모자를 만든 다음에 왜 병이 들었습니까?
c. 모자 장수가 죽은 다음 어떤 일이 일어났습니까?

Writing Activity

이 이야기에서 한 등장인물이 다른 선택을 했다면 이야기가 어떻게 달라질지 반 친구들이나 옆사람과 토론하십시오.

Discuss as a class or with a partner how the story might have changed if one character had made a different choice in the story.

The Pronunciation of Korean Sounds

1. Vowels

	sound		sound		sound		sound
아 a	as in "father"	야 ya	as in "yacht"	애	as in "sand"	얘 ye	as in "yet"
어 eo	as in "son"	여 yeo	as in "young"	에	as in "set"	예 ye	as in "yet"
오 o	as in "home"	요 yo	as in "yo-yo"	외	as in "wet"	와 wa	as in "watt"
우 u	as in "lute"	유 yu	as in "you/U"	위	as in "we"	워 weo	as in "won"
으 oo	as in "book"			의 üi	as in "wë"	왜 wae	as in "wet"
이 ee	as in "police"					웨 we	as in "wen"

2. Consonants

	sound		sound		sound		sound
ㄱ	k "kite"	ㅋ	k' "khaki"	ㄲ	kk "gum"	ㄴ	n "noon"
ㄷ	t "television"	ㅌ	t' "toe"	ㄸ	tt "dog'	ㄹ	l, r "run"
ㅂ	p "pool"	ㅍ	p' "pick"	ㅃ	pp "bird"	ㅁ	m "mom"
ㅅ	s "salad"			ㅆ	ss "sun"	ㅇ	ng "song"
ㅈ	ch "jam"	ㅊ	ch' "itch"	ㅉ	jj "joke"	ㅎ	h "happy"

Reading and Writing Korean

1. Vowels

Practice writing the vowels and saying them out loud ('ㅇ' is a silent place-holder before a vowel).

ㅏ	ㅏ				아				
ㅓ	ㅓ				어				
ㅗ	ㅗ				오				
ㅜ	ㅜ				우				
ㅡ	ㅡ				으				
ㅣ	ㅣ				이				
ㅑ	ㅑ				야				
ㅕ	ㅕ				여				
ㅛ	ㅛ				요				
ㅠ	ㅠ				유				

ㅐ	ㅐ				애				
ㅔ	ㅔ				에				
ㅚ	ㅚ				외				
ㅟ	ㅟ				위				
ㅢ	ㅢ				의				
ㅒ	ㅒ				얘				
ㅖ	ㅖ				예				
ㅘ	ㅘ				와				
ㅝ	ㅝ				워				
ㅙ	ㅙ				왜				
ㅞ	ㅞ				웨				

2. Consonants

Practice writing the consonants and saying them out loud.

ㄱ	ㄱ								
ㄴ	ㄴ								
ㄷ	ㄷ								
ㄹ	ㄹ								
ㅁ	ㅁ								
ㅂ	ㅂ								
ㅅ	ㅅ								
ㅇ	ㅇ								
ㅈ	ㅈ								
ㅊ	ㅊ								
ㅋ	ㅋ								

ㅌ	ㅌ								
ㅍ	ㅍ								
ㅎ	ㅎ								
ㄲ	ㄲ								
ㄸ	ㄸ								
ㅃ	ㅃ								
ㅆ	ㅆ								
ㅉ	ㅉ								

Creating Korean Syllables

1. If the vowel is vertical it will appear on the right or left of the consonant. Read the sounds by following the arrows and numbers.

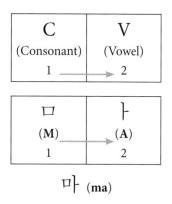

마 (ma)

Look back at the consonant and vowel charts to review these sounds, then try to sound out these syllables. The first three are done for you.

마	야	너	여	시	해	계	애	예
(ma)	(ya)	(no)						
마	야	너	여	시	해	계	애	예

2. If the vowel is horizontal, it will be above or below the consonant.

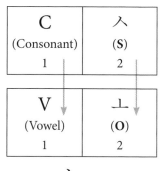

소 (so)

187

Look back at the consonant and vowel charts to review these sounds, then try to sound out these syllables. The first three are done.

소 (so)	요 (yo)	주 (ju)	류	그	우	유	고	뇨
소	요	주	류	그	우	유	고	뇨

3. For a syllable with multiple consonants and vertical vowels, follow the numbers in the box. Read the sounds by following the arrows and numbers.

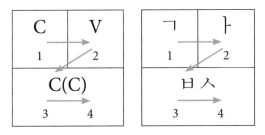

값 (**kaps**) A syllable with multiple consonants looks like this.

Try to sound out these syllables. The first three are done for you.

김 (kim)	감 (kam)	랑 (rang)	젊	많	값	달	떡	산
김	감	랑	젊	많	값	달	떡	산

4. For a syllable with multiple consonants and horizontal vowels, follow the numbers in the box. Read number 1 first, then number 2, then number 3 and so on.

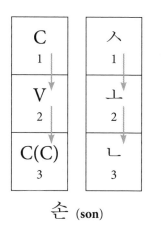

손 (son)

Try to sound out these syllables. The first three are done for you.

손	용	흙	울	금	은	곰	숲	혹
(son)	(yong)	(hulk)						
손	용	흙	울	금	은	곰	숲	혹

5. For syllables with single or no consonants read from box #1 then down, then over. Follow the numbers to form syllables.

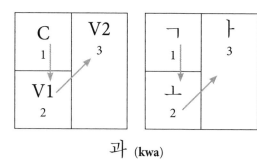

과 (kwa)

Try to sound out these syllables. The first one is done for you.

과 (gwa)	워	외	돼	꿰	쥐	귀	화	쇠
과	워	외	돼	꿰	쥐	귀	화	쇠

6. For syllables with multiple consonants and multiple vowels follow the numbers.

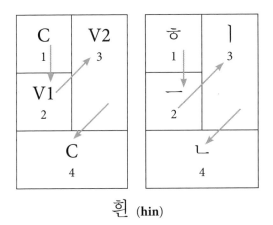

힌 (**hin**)

Try to sound out these syllables. The first one is done for you.

힌 (hin)	왕	원	왼	됐	웬	윈	된	광
힌	왕	원	왼	됐	웬	윈	된	광

Reading and Writing Korean Words

1. Practice reading and writing the following words that have syllables with vertical vowels.

자다 **jada** to sleep	다리 **dali** leg	여자 **yeoja** woman	아이 **ai** child
자 다	다 리	여 자	아 이

2. Practice reading and writing the following words that have syllables with horizontal vowels.

소 **so** cow	나무 **namu** tree	여우 **yeo-u** fox	토끼 **tokki** rabbit
소	나 무	여 우	토 끼

3. Practice reading and writing the following words that have syllables with both vertical vowels, horizontal vowels and multiple consonants.

달 **dal** the moon	떡 **tteog** rice cake	호랑이 **holangi** tiger	산 **san** mountain
달	떡	호랑이	산

4. Practice reading and writing the following words that have syllables with both vertical vowels, horizontal vowels and multiple consonants.

겨울 **gyeo-ul** winter	금 **geum** gold	은 **eun** silver	곰 **gom** bear
겨 울	금	은	곰

5. Practice reading and writing the following words that have syllables with both vertical vowels, horizontal vowels and multiple consonants.

금화 **geumhwa** golden coin	방귀 **bang-gui** a fart	돼지 **dwaeji** pig	쇠 **soe** steel
금 화	방 귀	돼 지	쇠

6. Practice reading and writing the following words that have syllables with both vertical vowels, horizontal vowels and multiple consonants.

원하다 **wonhada** to want	왕 **wang** king	흰색 **hinsak** white	왼쪽 left
원 하 다	왕	흰 색	왼 쪽

Pronunciation Activity

Write the syllables in the empty boxes and say the pairs.

1.

	VS.	
곰 **gom** bear		공 **gong** ball

2.

	VS.	
돈 **don** money		동 **dong** copper

3.

	VS.	
감 **gam** persimmon		강 **gang** river

4.

	VS.	
사람 **salam** person		사랑 **salang** love

5.

	VS.	
손 **son** hand		산 **san** mountain

6.

	VS.	
방 **bang** room		밤 **bam** night

7.

	VS.	
문 **mun** door		물 **mul** water

8.

	VS.		VS.	
달 **tal** month		딸 **ttal** daughter		탈 **tal** mask

9.

	VS.		VS.	
말 **mal** horse		발 **bal** foot		팔 **pal** arm

10.

	VS.		VS.	
불 **bul** fire		뿔 **bbul** horn		풀 **pul** grass

Reading and Writing Korean Sentences

1.

안	녕	하	세	요.
An	nyeong	ha	se	yo

Hello.

안	녕	하	세	요.

2.

반	갑	습	니	다.
ban	gab	seub	ni	da

Nice to meet you.

반	갑	습	니	다.

3.

고	맙	습	니	다.
go	mab	seub	ni	da

Thank you.

고	맙	습	니	다.

4.

죄	송	합	니	다.
joe	song	hab	ni	da

Sorry.

죄	송	합	니	다.

5.

실	례	합	니	다.
sil	lye	hab	ni	da

Excuse me.

실	례	합	니	다.

6.

안	녕	히	가	세	요.
an	nyeong	hi	ga	se	yo

Goodbye.

안	녕	히	가	세	요.

7.

제		이	름	은		소
je		i	leum	eun		so

My name is Sophia.

제		이	름	은		소

피	아	입	니	다.
pi	a	ib	ni	da

피	아	입	니	다.

8.

저	는	미	국	사	람	입	니	다.
jeo	neun	mi	gug	sa	lam	ib	ni	da

I am American.

저	는	미	국	사	람	입	니	다.

9.

저	는		학	생	입	니	다.
jeo	neun		hag	saeng	ib	ni	da

I am a student.

저	는		학	생	입	니	다.

10.

옛	날	에		소	년	이	있	었	습	니	다.
yes	nal	e		so	nyeon	i	iss	eoss	seub	ni	da

Once upon a time, there was a boy.

옛	날	에		소	년	이	있	었	습	니	다.

11.

나	무	꾼	이		말	했	습	니	다.
na	mu	kkun	i		mal	haess	seub	ni	da

Said the woodcutter.

나	무	꾼	이		말	했	습	니	다.

12.

그	가		죽	었	습	니	다.
geu	ga		jug	eoss	seub	ni	da

He died.

그	가		죽	었	습	니	

13.

그	녀	는		착	했	습	니	다.
geu	nyeo	neun		chag	haess	seub	ni	da

She was nice.

그	녀	는		착	했	습	니	다.

14.

그	는		화	가		났	습	니	다.
geu	neun		hwa	ga		nass	seub	ni	da

He was angry.

그	는		화	가		났	습	니	다.

15.

그	녀	는		매	우		슬	펐	습	니	다.
geu	nyeo	neun		mae	u		seul	peoss	seub	ni	da

She was very sad.

그	녀	는		매	우		슬	펐	습	니	다.

16.

그	가	그	돌	을		먹	었	습	니	다.
geu	ga	geu	dol	eul		meog	eoss	seub	ni	da

He ate the stone.

그	가	그	돌	을		먹	었	습	니	다.

17.

그	녀	가			울	었	습	니	다.
geu	nyeo	ga			ul	eoss	seub	ni	da

She cried.

그	녀	가			울	었	습	니	다.

18.

그	의	이	름	은	견	우	입	니	다.
geu	ui	i	leum	eun	gyeon	u	ib	ni	da

His name is Gyeon-u.

그	의	이	름	은	견	우	입	니	다.

19.

그	녀	는	달	이	되	었	습	니	다.
geu	nyeo	neun	dal	i	doe	eoss	seub	ni	da

She became the moon.

그	녀	는	달	이	되	었	습	니	다.

20.

행	복	하	게	살	았	습	니	다.
haeng	bog	ha	ge	sal	ass	seub	ni	da

(He/She) lived happily ever after.

행	복	하	게	살	았	습	니	다.

Korean to English Glossary

Meeting New Friends

안녕하세요	hello	사람	a person
제	my	반갑습니다	nice to meet you
이름	name	한국	Korea
저	I	씨	Mr. (or Mrs.)
미국	America	안녕히 가세요	goodbye

My Friends, Minsu

학생	a student	먹다	to eat
아침	morning	가다	to go
일찍	early	만나다	to meet
아침밥	breakfast	인사하다	to greet
학교	a school	공부	to study

The Fox Who is the King of Animals 동물의 왕 여우

동물	an animal	무섭다	scared
왕	a king	하지만	however
여우	a fox	말하다	to say
어느 날	one day	믿지 않다	to not believe
숲 속	in the forest	뒤	behind
걷다	to walk	따라오다	to follow
갑자기	suddenly	보다	to see
호랑이	a tiger	달아나다	to run away
나타나다	to appear	믿다	to believe

The Tiger Who Bowed to the Chestnut 밤에게 절을 한 호랑이

어느 날	one day	아주	very, so
호랑이	a tiger	아프다	to hurt
산 속	in the mountains	먹을 수 없다	cannot eat
걷다	to walk	계속	still
배가 고프다	hungry	밤송이	chestnut burr
그때	at that time	~라고 생각하다	to think something
고슴도치	a hedgehog	무섭다	scared
보다	to see	그래서	so
깨물다	to bite	절을 하다	to bow
가시	quill		

A Sleepyhead Baby Bear 잠꾸러기 아기 곰

아기 곰	a baby bear	씻지 않다	to not wash
숲 속에	in the forest	얼굴	a face
늦게 잤다	to sleep late (past tense)	갔다	to go (past tense)
학교	a school	연못	a pond
늦게 갔다	to go late (past tense)	깨끗해지다	to become clean
반 친구들	classmates	웃다	to smile
놀리다	to tease		

The Donkey and the Grasshopper   당나귀와 메뚜기

메뚜기	a grasshopper	물어보다	to ask
노래를 부르다	to sing	먹다	to eat
나무	a tree	이슬	dew
당나귀	a donkey	며칠 뒤	a few days later
노래를 잘 하다	to sing well	아프다	to get sick
원하다	to want	죽다	to die

The Tiger and the Rabbit   호랑이와 토끼

배고프다	to be hungry	나중에	later
호랑이	a tiger	기다리다	to wait
토끼	a rabbit	가져오다	to bring
원하다	to want	돌	a stone
먹다	to eat	굽다	a grill
주다	to give	뜨겁다	to be hot
따뜻한 떡	a warm rice cake	울다	to cry

A Father and His Two Daughters   아버지와 그의 두 딸들

농부	a farmer	질문	a question
도예가	a potter	날씨	weather
소원	a wish	화창하다	sunny
농장	a farm	기도하다	to pray
비	rain	원하다	to wish
똑같은	same		

The Farting Match   방귀 시합

방귀	a fart	하자고 하다	to say let's do something
시합	a match		
두 명	two people	항아리	a pot
한 명	one person	방귀를 꾸다	to fart
여자	a woman	쪽	side
남자	a man	날아가다	to fly
서로	each other	하루 종일	all day long
다른	different	아무도	nobody
마을	a village	이기다	to win
집	a house	포기하다	to give up
살다	to live		

The Sun and the Moon   해님 달님

어머니	a mother	집	a house
돈	money	꼬리	tail
아들	a son	먹다	to eat
딸	a daughter	입다	to wear
호랑이	a tiger	밖	outside
숲	a forest	나무	a tree
나타나다	to appear	자르다	to cut down
떡	rice cake	기도하다	to pray
옷	clothes	하늘	heaven

줄	a rope	해	sun
망가지다	to break	달	moon
떨어지다	to fall	올라가다	to climb

The Filial Tiger 효자 호랑이

나무꾼	a woodcutter	베다	to cut down
무서워하다	to be scared	호랑이	a tiger
거짓말	to lie	말하다	to say
태어나다	to be born	형제	a sibling
멧돼지	a boar	죽다	to die
믿다	to believe	보내주다	to let someone go
효자	filial	한 달	one month
슬픔	grief	가져다주다	to bring
옛날에	once upon a time	며칠	couple of days

The Tiger and the Dried Persimmon 호랑이와 곶감

산	a mountain	밖	outside
작다	small	아이	a child
마을	a village	울다	to cry
호랑이	a tiger	엄마	a mother
겨울	winter	여우	a fox
저녁	evening	곰	a bear
배고프다	hungry	먹다	to eat
찾다	to find	무섭다	scary
음식	food	실망하다	disappointed
집	a house	도망가다	to run away

Three-Years Hill 삼 년 고개

노인	an old man	걱정하다	to worry
살다	to live	소년	a little boy
작은 마을	a small village	방문하다	to visit
언덕	a hill	똑똑하다	to be wise
넘어지다	to fall down	해결책	a solution
삼 년	three years	삼 십	thirty
걷다	to walk	웃다	to laugh
조심하다	to be careful	함께	together
슬프다	to be sad	즐기다	to enjoy
눕다	to lay down	절대~않다	never
침대	a bed		

The Old Man with the Lump 혹부리 할아버지

혹부리	a person with a lump	밤	night
할아버지	an old man	무섭다	scary
목	neck	노래를 부르다	to sing
혹	a lump	오다	to come
산	a mountain	아름답다	to be beautiful
나무를 하다	to cut wood	도깨비	a goblin
집에 오는 길	on one's way home	어디	where

나오다	to come out	부자	a rich person
가져가다	to take away	행복하다	to be happy
돈	money	살다	to live

Two Brothers Who Threw Away Their Lumps of Gold   금덩이를 버린 형제

옛날에	a long time ago	형	an older brother
두–	two	배	a boat
형제	brothers	갑자기	suddenly
서로 좋아하다	to like each other	던지다	to throw
남동생	a younger brother	~속으로	into
찾다	to find	에 대해 생각하다	to think about
덩이	lumps	훔치다	to steal
금	gold	욕심이 많다	to be greedy
물	water	자랑스럽다	to be proud
주다	to give		

The Golden Ax and the Silver Ax   금도끼와 은도끼

둘	two	신	a god
친구들	friends	은	silver
게으르다	lazy	금	gold
욕심이 많다	greedy	쇠	iron
산	a mountain	정직함	honesty
자르다/베다	to cut	질투하다	jealous
나무	wood/tree	화가 나다	to be mad
떨어뜨리다	to drop	받다	to receive
빠지다	to fall	치다	to hit
연못	a pond	머리	head

Heungboo and Nolbu   흥부와 놀부

형제	brothers	낫다	to get better
돈	money	날아가다	to fly away
욕심	greedy	세	three
관대	generous	씨앗	seeds
새	a bird	금화	gold coins
깨진 다리	a broken leg	도망가다	to run away
돕는다	to help	자르다	to cut
집	a house	악마	devil

The Story of Gyeon-Uh and Jik-Nyeo   견우와 직녀

공주	a princess	화가 나다	to be mad
하늘	heaven	떨어뜨리다	to separate
이름	name	동쪽	east
농부	a farmer	서쪽	west
왕	a king	보다	to see
좋아하지 않다	to not like	울다	to cry
관계	relationship	매일	every day
좋아하다	to like	안타까워 하다	to feel sorry
서로	each other	허락하다	to allow

만나다	to meet	도와주다	to help
일 년에 한 번	once a year	다리	a bridge
까마귀 떼	crows	비	rain
까치 떼	magpies		

Stupid On-Dal and Princess Pyeong-Gang   바보 온달과 평강공주

남자	a man	원하다	to want
이름	a name	화가 나다	to be mad
사람들	people	쫓아내다	to kick out
생각하다	to think	배우다	to learn
바보	a stupid person	양궁	archery
작은	little	문학	literature
공주	a princess	이웃 나라	a neighboring country
울다	to cry	침략하다	to invade
결혼하다	to marry	도망가다	to run away
되다	to become	죽이다	to kill
어른	an adult	칭찬하다	to praise
똑똑하다	smart	상을 주다	to reward

The Lazy Boy Who Became a Cow   소가 된 게으름뱅이

소년	a boy	가면	a mask
싫어하다	to hate	마법이 있는	magical
일하다	to work	쓰다	to wear (a mask)
눕다	to lay down	흥분하다	to be excited
사람들	people	힘들다	to be hard
게으르다	lazy	고통스럽다	to be painful
먹다	to eat	그리워하다	to miss somebody
저녁	dinner	채찍질하다	to whip
침대	a bed	꿈을 꾸다	to dream
소	a cow	후회하다	to regret
신경쓰다	to care about	변하다	to change
자다	to sleep	부지런하다	to be diligent
노인	an old man	듣다	to listen
방문하다	to visit		

The Mouse in the Shape of a Man   사람으로 둔갑한 쥐

옛날 옛날에	once upon a time	손톱	a fingernail
사람	a man	갑자기	suddenly
공부	studying	계속	to keep
아무도 없다	there is no one	기다리다	to wait
아주	really/very	섭섭하다	to be sad/ disappointed
외롭다	to be lonely		
어느 날	one day	돌아가다	to go back/return
쥐	a mouse	똑같이 생기다	to look the same
마리	counter for animals	놀라다	to be surprised
놀러 오다	to visit (lit., to come to play)	가족	family
		~들	plural for nouns
음식	food	가짜	an imposter/a fake

내쫓다	to throw someone out	물어뜯다	to bite
기도하다	to pray	변하다	to be changed
고양이	a cat		

The Half Son 반쪽 아들

부부	a married couple	파다	to dig
나이가 많다	to be old	버드나무	a willow tree
자식	children	바위	a rock
백일 동안	for 100 days	앞마당	a front yard
아들	a son	번쩍 들다	to lift something easily
낳다	to give birth	결혼	marriage
눈	an eye	부모님	parents
귀	an ear	몰래	secretly
팔	an arm	묶다	to tie
다리	a leg	소리치다	to yell out
반쪽	half (side)	데려가다	to bring (a person)
신기하다	miraculous	반대쪽	opposite side
능력	power	하룻밤	one night
우물	a well		

The Story Ghost 이야기 귀신

이야기	a story	되다	to become
아이	a child (boy or girl)	전날	a day before
하지만	but/however	놀다	to play
듣다	to listen	잠들다	to fall asleep
~만	only ~	깨다	to awake
남	others	배	a pear
들려 주다	to tell	다른	different
적다	to write	바늘	a needle
주머니	a pocket	방석	a cushion
넣어 두다	to put something in	걱정	a concern
자라다	to grow up	따라가다	to follow
총각	a bachelor	밀다	to push
오래	for a long time	넘어지다	to fall down
귀신	a ghost		

The Freshwater Snail Bride 우렁이 신부

하지 못하다	cannot do something	점심	lunch
노총각	an old bachelor	차려져 있다	to be prepared (food)
외롭다	to be lonely	궁금하다	to be curious
일	to work/a work	배가 고프다	to be hungry
혼자	alone	그냥	just because
누구/누군가	someone	~척 하다	to pretend ~
같이	together	부엌	a kitchen
먹고 살다	to live (lit., eat and live)	숨다	to hide
대답하다	to answer	예쁘다	to be pretty
소리	a sound	변하다	to be changed
우렁이	a freshwater snail	다시	again

또	again	여자	woman
일하러 가다	to go to work	행복하게 살다	to live happily
그러자	then/and then		

The Fairy and the Woodcutter　선녀와 나무꾼

나무꾼	a woodcutter	보름달	a full moon
그때	at that time	뜨다	to rise (the moon or
사슴	a deer		sun)
뛰어오다	to run (to someone)	연못	a pond
숨겨 주다	to hide (someone)	선녀	a fairy (Taoist fairy)
사냥꾼	a hunter	목욕	a bath
쫓아오다	to chase	제일	the most
보다	to see	예쁘다	to be beautiful
못	can't do	날개옷	a robe of feathers
모르는 척 하다	to pretend you don't	다시	again
	know	돌아가다	to go back
저 쪽	that way	낳다	to give birth
거짓말	a lie	부르다	to call
믿다	to believe	업다	to carry (someone) on
고맙다고 하다	to say thank you		your back

The Fox and the Old Woman　여우와 할머니

형제	brothers	무덤	a grave
욕심	greed	깨다	to be awakened from
많다	to be a lot		sleep
착하다	to be kind	여우	a fox
부모님	the parents	해골	a skull
돌아가시다	to die (honorific)	머리	a head
다	all of ~	쓰다	to wear
가져가다	to take, to bring	재주를 넘다	to do cartwheels
아무것도 주지 않다	to give nothing	할머니	an old woman
그래서	therefore	도착하다	to arrive
여기저기	from here to there	막대기	a stick
돌아다니다	to wander	지나가다	to pass by
소금	salt	때리다	to hit
장사	a sale	보살펴 주다	to take care of someone

The Beggar Brothers　거지 형제

어렸을 때	when you were young	큰 집	a big house
여기저기	from here to there	작은 집	a small house
돌아다니다	to wander	동네	a village
얻어먹다	to beg for food (and eat	~만 있는 …	… that only has ~
	it)	착한 ~	a nice ~ (person)
아주	very	그대로 하다	to do as one is told
욕심이 많다	to be greedy	그런데	however
욕심이 많아서	because you are greedy	그 날	on that particular day
자기보다 더 많이	more than oneself	다들	everyone
화를 내다	to get angry	아프다	to be sick

아파서	because you are sick
문	a door
열다	to open
집집마다	at every house
잔치	a (traditional) party
다시/또	again
끝나서	because it is ended/ over
아프지 않으려고	to avoid getting sick

The *Hwasubun* Bowl 화수분 바가지

가난하다	to be poor
농사꾼	a farmer
가난하지만	although you are poor
아주	very
농사	farming
잘 되지 않다	to not be working well
먹을 것	something to eat
없다	there is nothing/no one
사다	to buy
밖에 나가다	to go outside
어떤 사람	a person, someone
잔뜩	a lot of
잡다	to catch
묻다	to ask
어디에 쓰려고	to use it for something
불쌍하다	to be poor, pathetic
돈	money
전부	all, every
넣어 주다	to put
개굴개굴	ribbit ribbit
바가지	a bowl
한 컵	a (one) cupful
넣다	to put it into somewhere
계속	a (traditional) party
생겨나다	to continue to grow
은혜를 갚다	to repay one's kindness
나누어 주다	to pass around, share

The Net Bag for Catching a Tiger 호랑이 잡는 망태기

망태기	a net bag
가난하다	to be poor
총각	a single man
찾다	to find
산으로	to the mountain
밤	the night
~이 되고 말다	to become … (negative)
발견하다	to discover/to find
할아버지	an old man/ grandfather
하룻밤	one night
하룻밤만	only one night
자다	to sleep
자고 가다	to sleep over
들어오다	to come in
짚	a straw
만들다	to make
만들고 있다	to be making
왜	why
여기	here
많아지다	to pile up
귀가 솔깃해지다	to be very interested
~어/아도 될까요?	May I ~?
입구	an entrance/mouth of a bag
꽉 묶다	to tie up tightly
나뭇가지	a branch
소리를 지르다	to scream
뾰족하다	to be sharp, pointy

The Red Fan and the Blue Fan 빨간 부채 파란 부채

빨간 부채	a red fan
파란 부채	a blue fan
욕심쟁이	a greedy person
부자	a rich person
손님	a guest/visitor
찾아오다	to visit
재워 주다	to let someone stay
아깝다	to grudge something
열어 주지 않다	do not open
새로	newly
깨끗하다	to be clean
방	a room
방으로 안내하다	to show a person to a room
다음 날 아침	the next morning
사라지다	to disappear

(부채를) 부치다	to wave (a fan)
코	a nose
길어지다	to grow longer
짧아지다	to become shorter
가지고 다니다	to carry with
가지고 싶다	to want to have
계속	to keep (doing something)
하늘	the sky
위	the top/above
신령	God/deity
그것도 모르고	to be unaware of something (negative)
화가 풀리다	the anger is melted away

The Salt Millstone   소금 맷돌

농사꾼	a farmer
조금	a little bit / some
맷돌	a millstone
가지다	to have
쓰러지다	to fall down
쓰러져 있다	to have fallen
데려오다	to bring (a person)
따뜻하다	to be warm
고마워하다	to appreciate
하지만	but/however
그냥	just/just because/simply
돌리다	to spin
생각하다	to think
그러자	then/and then
~았/었으면 좋겠다	it would be great if ~
나오다	to come out
이웃 사람들	the neighbors
소문	some news/a rumor
도둑	a thief
훔치다	to steal
바다	the sea
그 때	at that time
소금	salt
비싸다	to be expensive
무거워지다	to become heavy
가라앉다	to sink
짜지다	to be salty

The Magpie That Repaid Kindness   은혜 갚은 까치

은혜	kindness
갚다	to repay
까치	a magpie
산 너머 마을	a village across a mountain
길	a street
뱀	a snake
마리	counter noun for animals
잡아먹다	to prey on
돕다	to help
활	a bow
쏘다	to shoot
그리고 나서	after that
주인	an owner
숨이 막히다	to find it hard to breathe
내	my
남편	a husband
만약	if
열두 시	12 o'clock
전에	before
절	a temple
종	a bell
세 번	three times
울리다	to ring
살려 주다	to spare one's life
깊은 밤	to be late into the night
피를 흘리다	to bleed
묻다	to bury/be stained with

The Rat-Snake Scholar   구렁이 선비

구렁이	a rat snake
선비	a scholar
징그럽다	to be gross
구석	a corner
자매	sisters
구경	to explore, sightsee
쿡쿡 찌르다	to poke
눈물	the tears
가엾다	to be pitiful
닦아 주다	to wipe away

결혼하고 싶다	to want to marry	과거 시험	a civil service exam
아궁이	a fireplace	허물	a snakeskin
허락	an approval, permission	비단	silk (fabric)
옷	clothes	억지로	to be against one's will
잘 차려 입다	to dress up well	까마귀	a crow
멋지다	to be cool	벌레	a bug
배가 아프다 (an idiom)	to feel envious	돼지	a boar
		빨래	laundry
		젓가락	chopsticks
전염병	an infectious disease	노를 젓다	to row

The Toad That Repaid Kindness 은혜 갚은 두꺼비

두꺼비	a toad	여자	a woman
부엌	a kitchen	신	the god
밥을 푸다	to scoop rice	바치다	to offer (a sacrifice)
엉금엉금	to crawl	바쳐지다	to be offered (as a sacrifice)
기어들어오다	to crawl into		
쳐다보다	to look	전날 저녁	the evening before
아이구	oh, oops	멈추다	to stop
불쌍하다	to be pathetic	마침내	finally
한 주걱	one scoop	천장	a ceiling
밥그릇	a rice bowl	지네	a centipede
그 다음부터	from then on	왕지네	a big centipede
점점 커지다	to get bigger and bigger	뛰어오르다	to jump up
그러던 어느 날	then one day	쫓아 버리다	to drive away
전염병	an infectious disease	불태워 죽이다	to burn to death

The Manic Goblin 정신없는 도깨비

정신없다	to be manic	연기처럼 사라지다	to disappear without a trace
도깨비	a goblin		
태어나자마자	right after you were born	공짜로	for nothing, for free
		몇 달	a few months
외롭다	to be lonely	찌그러지다	to be dented
또래	about the same age as you	냄비	a pot
		요술	magic
꼬마	a little boy	다듬이방망이	a laundry bat
손뼉을 치다	to clap	도깨비 방망이	a goblin bat (a magical bat)
두 번	twice		
기분이 나빠지다	to feel bad	두드리다	to beat
아무렇지 않은 척 하다	to pretend to be calm	이불	a blanket
		훌쩍 훌쩍 울다	to weep, shed a few tears
돈을 빌리다	to lend money	죄	a sin
돈을 갚다	to pay back money	벌을 받다	to be punished
쫄쫄 굶다	to skip a meal entirely	이제까지	until now

A Single Grain of Millet 좁쌀 한 알

좁쌀	millet	밟다	to stomp on
똑똑하다	to be smart	외양간	a cow barn
구하다	to find/to seek	소	a cow
여행을 떠나다	to go off on a journey	뿔	a horn
한 알	a single grain	받다	to receive/to butt
가지고 있다	to take, to have	팔다	to sell
돌려주다	to give back, return	팔리다	to be sold
어젯밤	last night	정승	a minister
다른	to be different, another	생일	a birthday
~이어/아야만 하다	it should be ~	생일 잔치	a birthday party
당황하다	to be embarrassed	하인	a servant
고양이	a cat	설명하다	to explain
마구간	a horse barn	이미	already
말	a horse		

The Three Brothers 삼형제

세 가지	three kinds of	돌아오다	to come back
유산	legacy	짓다	to build
삼형제	the three brothers	왼쪽	left
담뱃대	a pipe	가운데	middle
맷돌	a millstone	오른쪽	right
장구	a double-headed drum	밤새	all night
장례식	a funeral	냄새	a smell
나이가 많다	to be older	맡다	to smell
힘이 세다	to be strong	갈림길	a crossroad
(장구를) 잘 치다	to be good at playing	목말을 타다	to stand on one's shoulders
걷다	to walk		
세 갈래	to be three-forked	신이 나다	to become excited
헤어지다	to part	어깨	a shoulder
돈을 벌다	to earn money	무너지다	to collapse

The Treasure Given by a Goblin 도깨비가 준 보물

보물	a treasure	아무것도 모르다	to know nothing
콩	a bean	엉덩이	one's backside
보리	a barley	금	gold
더하기	plus	똥	poop
조금	a little bit	출발하다	to start on one's way
모자라다	to be a fool	절대로	never
세상 구경	sightseeing the world	안 되다	should not do
가방	a bag	그래서	therefore, thus
빈 집	an empty house	그랬더니	then
보자기	a wrapping cloth	마구	severely
그것도 모르고	without knowing it	잘못하다	to do wrong
자랑을 하다	to show off	저번에	last time
한숨을 쉬다	to sigh	제발	please
야단치다	to scold		

A Painting That will make Your Wishes Come True   소원을 들어주는 그림

소원	a wish	항아리	a pot
들어 주다	to grant a wish	두드리다	to knock
나누다	to split/share	상자	a box
서로	each other	스무 번	twenty times
시골	the countryside	서른 번	thirty times
서울	Seoul	마흔 번	forty times
굶다	not able to eat anything	왕궁	the palace
여행하다	to travel	창고	a warehouse
불행하다	to be unhappy	잡아오다	to catch and bring a person
진작	already/sooner	잡혀오다	to be caught and brought
그림	a painting		
황새	a crane	사형 날짜	the day of execution
하루	one day (time period)	채찍	a whip
다리	a leg		
부러지다	to be broken		

A Fake Expert Archer   가짜 명궁

서른	thirty (years of age)	큰소리를 치다	to talk through his hat (make noise)
넘다	to be over, past		
논	a rice paddy	눈앞이 캄캄하다	to be hopeless (idiom)
밭	a field of grain	단번에	only once
무작정	thoughtlessly	비틀다	to wring
장사	a business	순식간에	quickly
어리숙하다	to be naïve	대회	a tournament
겉모습	an appearance, look	과녁	a target
좋은 대접	a good treatment	정중앙	the center
푸대접	a poor treatment	활시위를 당기다	to draw back the bow-string
꿩	a pheasant		
명궁	an expert archer	재촉하다	to rush
정승	the government minister	마침	just in time
		감탄하다	to amaze/admire at
부엉이	an owl	망치다	to mess up/spoil

The Taming of the Mother-in-Law   시어머니 길들이기

시어머니	a mother-in-law	친정	a married woman's parents' home
길들이기	the taming		
괴롭히다	to harass	소문이 나다	to be in the air
빠르다	to be fast	회초리	a cane
느리다	to be slow	버릇을 고치다	to correct one's bad habit
며느리	a daughter-in-law		
엎지르다	to spill	사정없이	severely
말버릇이 나쁘다	to have a foul mouth	어이가 없다	to be dumbfounded
기다렸다는 듯이	like one was waiting for	미치다	to be crazy
얼굴색 한번 바꾸지 않고	without changing countenance	대성통곡	to wail
		그럴듯하다	to be plausible
시아버지	a father-in-law	속이 새까맣게 타다	to eat oneself up
보기가 힘들다	too difficult to see	실컷	as much as one likes

떠들고 다니다	to talk about it everywhere	사과하다	to apologize
잘못하다	to do wrong	효도하다	to do one's filial duty

The King Has Donkey's Ears 임금님 귀는 당나귀 귀

임금님	a king (*honorific form*)	바치다	to dedicate
걱정	a worry	날이 갈수록	as days go by
귀	an ear	입이 근질근질하다	to be full of news
쑥쑥 자라다	to become bigger	똑같다	to be the same
당나귀	a donkey	차라리	rather than
사흘	three days	대나무	a bamboo tree
이만큼	this much	십 년 묵은 체증이 내려가다	a huge weight has been lifted off one's chest
거울	a mirror		
존경받다	to be honored	한꺼번에	at once
핑계	an excuse	앓던 이가 빠지는 것 같다	to feel sudden relief
평생	for the rest of one's life		
모자 장수	a hatter	명령하다	to order
엎드리다	to lie face down	동백나무	a camellia tree
가능한 빨리	as soon as possible	뽑아 버리다	to root up
감쪽같다	to be just as it was		

English to Korean Glossary

For ease of search, all verb meanings are listed under T: "to ~", "to be/become ~."

… that only has ~	~만 있는
… 12 o'clock	열두 시

A

a few days later	며칠 뒤
a few months	몇 달
about the same age as you	또래
adult	어른
after that	그리고 나서
again	다시 / 또
against one's will	억지로
all	전부
all day long	하루 종일
all night	밤새
all of ~	다
alone	혼자
already	이미
already/sooner	진작
although you are poor	가난하지만
America	미국
anger is melted away	화가 풀리다
animal	동물
appearance, look	겉모습
approval	허락
approval, permission	허락
archery	양궁
arm	팔
as days go by	날이 갈수록
as much as one likes	실컷
as soon as possible	가능한 빨리
at every house	집집마다
at once	한꺼번에
at that time	그때
awake	깨다

B

baby bear	아기 곰
bachelor	총각
bag	가방
bamboo tree	대나무
barley	보리

bath	목욕
bean	콩
bear	곰
beat	두드리다
beautiful	아름답다
because it is ended/over	끝나서
because you are greedy	욕심이 많아서
because you are sick	아파서
bed	침대
before	전에
behind	뒤
bell	종
big centipede	왕지네
big house	큰 집
bird	새
birthday	생일
birthday party	생일 잔치
blanket	이불
blue fan	파란 부채
boar	멧돼지
boat	배
bow	활
bowl	바가지
box	상자
boy	소년
branch	나뭇가지
breakfast	아침밥
bridge	다리
broken leg	부러진 다리
brothers	형제
bug	벌레
business	장사
but/however	하지만
butt	받다

C

camellia tree	동백나무
cane	회초리
cannot do something	하지 못하다
cannot eat	먹을 수 없다

cannot eat anything	굶다
can't do	못
cat	고양이
ceiling	천장
center	정중앙
centipede	지네
chestnut burr	밤송이
child (boy or girl)	아이
children	자식
chopsticks	젓가락
civil service exam	과거 시험
classmates	반 친구들
clothes	옷
clothing	옷
concern	걱정
continued to grow	생겨나다
continuously	계속
corner	구석
counter noun for animals	마리
countryside	시골
couple of days	며칠
cow	소
cow barn	외양간
crane	황새
crossroad	갈림길
crow	까마귀
crows	까마귀 떼
cushion	방석

D

daughter	딸
daughter-in-law	며느리
day before	전날
day of execution	사형 날짜
deer	사슴
deity/God	신령
devil	악마
dew	이슬
different	다른
difficult to see	보기가 힘들다
diligent	부지런하다
dinner	저녁
disappointed	실망하다
do not open	열어 주지 않다
donkey	당나귀
door	문
double-headed drum	장구 활시위를

E

each other	서로
ear	귀
early	일찍
east	동쪽
empty house	빈 집
entrance/mouth of a bag	입구
evening	저녁
evening before the day	전날 저녁
every day	매일
everyone	다들
excited	흥분하다
excuse	핑계
expert archer	명궁
eye	눈

F

face	얼굴
fairy (Taoist fairy)	선녀
family	가족
farm	농장
farmer	농부/농사꾼
farming	농사
fart	방귀
father-in-law	시아버지
field	밭
filial	효자
finally	마침내
fingernail	손톱
fireplace	아궁이
food	음식
for 100 days	백일 동안
for a long time	오래
for not being sick	아프지 않으려고
for nothing, for free	공짜로
for the rest of one's life	평생
forest	숲
forty times	마흔 번
fox	여우
freshwater snail	우렁이
friends	친구들
from here to there	여기저기
from then on	그 다음부터
front yard	앞마당
full moon	보름달
funeral	장례식

G

generous	관대
ghost	귀신
goblin	도깨비
goblin bat (a magical bat)	도깨비 방망이
god	신
God/deity	신령
gold	금
gold coins	금화
goodbye	안녕히 가세요
good treatment	좋은 대접
government minister	정승
grandfather	할아버지
grandmother	할머니
grasshopper	메뚜기
grave	무덤
greed	욕심
greedy	욕심이 많다
greedy person	욕심쟁이
grief	슬픔
grill	굽다
guest/visitor	손님

H

half (side)	반쪽
hard	힘들다
hatter	모자 장수
head	머리
heaven	하늘/천국
hedgehog	고슴도치
hello	안녕하세요
here	여기
hill	언덕
honesty	정직함
horn	뿔
horse	말
horse barn	마구간
hot	뜨겁다
house	집
however	하지만/그런데
huge weight has been lifted off one's chest	십 년 묵은 체증이 내려가다
hungry	배가 고프다/ 배고프다
hunter	사냥꾼
husband	남편

I

I	저
if	만약
imposter/fake	가짜
infectious disease	전염병
into	~속으로
iron	쇠
it should be ~	~이어/아야만 하다
it would be great if ~	~았/었으면 좋겠다

J

just/just because/ simply	그냥
just in time	마침

K

kindness	은혜
king	왕
king (honorific form)	임금님
kitchen	부엌
Korea	한국

L

last night	어젯밤
last time	저번에
later	나중에
laundry	빨래
laundry bat	다듬이방망이
lazy	게으르다
left	왼쪽
leg	다리
legacy	유산
lie	거짓말
like one was waiting for	기다렸다는 듯이
literature	문학
little	작은
little bit	조금
little boy	소년/꼬마
long time ago	옛날에
lots of	잔뜩
lump	혹/덩이/덩어리
lunch	점심

M

magic	요술
magical	마법이 있는
magpie	까치
magpies	까치 떼

man	남자/사람	old woman	할머니
marriage	결혼	older brother	형
married couple	부부	on one's way home	집에 오는 길
married woman's	친정	on that particular day	그 날
parents' home		once a year	일 년에 한 번
mask	가면	once upon a time	옛날 옛날에 /
match	시합		옛날에
may I ~?	~어/아도 될까요?	one cupful	한 컵
middle	가운데	one day	어느 날
millet	좁쌀	one day	하루
millstone	맷돌	(time period)	
miraculous	신기하다	one month	한 달
mirror	거울	one night	하룻밤
money	돈	one person	한 명
moon	달	one scoop	한 주걱
more than oneself	자기보다 더 많이	one's backside	엉덩이
morning	아침	only ~	~만
(the) most	제일	only once	단번에
mother	어머니 / 엄마	only one night	하룻밤만
mother-in-law	시어머니	opposite side	반대쪽
mountain	산	others	남
mouse	쥐	outside	밖
Mr. (or Mrs.)	씨	owl	부엉이
should not do	안 되다	owner	주인
my	제 (hon.) / 내		

N

name	이름	**P**	
neck	목	painful	고통스럽다
needle	바늘	painting	그림
neighboring country	이웃 나라	palace	왕궁
neighbors	이웃 사람들	parents	부모님
net bag	망태기	pear	배
never	절대~않다/절대로	people	사람들
newly	새로	person	사람
news/rumor	소문	person with a lump	혹부리
next morning	다음 날 아침	person, someone	어떤 사람
nice ~ (person)	착한 ~	pheasant	꿩
nice to meet you	반갑습니다	pig	돼지
night	밤	pipe	담뱃대
nobody	아무도	please	제발
nose	코	plural for nouns	~들

O

		plus	더하기
		pocket	주머니
oh, oops	아이구	pond	연못
old	늙다	poop	똥
old bachelor	노총각	poor treatment	푸대접
old man	할아버지 / 노인	pot	항아리 / 냄비
		potter	도예가
		power	능력

prickle	가시	silk (fabric)	비단
princess	공주	silver	은
proud	자랑스럽다	sin	죄
Q		single grain of	한 알
question	질문	sisters	자매
quickly	순식간에	skull	해골
R		sky	하늘
rabbit	토끼	small	작다
rain	비	small house	작은 집
rather than	차라리	small village	작은 마을
rat snake	구렁이	smell	냄새/(냄새)맡다
really/very	아주	snake	뱀
red fan	빨간 부채	snakeskin	허물
relationship	관계	so	그래서
ribbit ribbit	개굴개굴	so	아주
rice bowl	밥그릇	solution	해결책
rice cake	떡	some	조금
rice paddy	논	someone	누구/누군가
rich person	부자	something to eat	먹을 것
right	오른쪽	son	아들
right after you were born	태어나자마자	sound	소리
		stick	막대기
robe of feathers	날개옷	still	계속
rock	바위	stone	돌
room	방	story	이야기
rope	줄	straw	짚
S		street	길
sad	슬프다	student	학생
sale	장사	study/studying	공부
salt	소금	stupid person	바보
same	똑같은	suddenly	갑자기
scared	무섭다/무서워하다	sun	해
scholar	선비	**T**	
school	학교	tail	꼬리
sea	바다	taming	길들이기
secretly	몰래	target	과녁
seeds	씨앗	tears	눈물
Seoul	서울	temple	절
servant	하인	that way	저 쪽
severely	마구/사정없이	the mountain	산으로
shoulder	어깨	then	그랬더니
sibling	형제	then/and then	그러자
side	쪽	then one day	그러던 어느 날
sightseeing	구경	there is no one	아무도 없다
sightseeing the world	세상 구경	there is nothing	없다
		therefore, thus	그래서
		thief	도둑

thirty	삼 십	to be gross	징그럽다
thirty (years of age)	서른	to be happy	행복하다
thirty times	서른 번	to be hard to breathe	숨이 막히다
this much	이만큼	to be having	가지고 있다
thoughtlessly	무작정	to be honored	존경받다
three	세	to be hopeless (*idiom*)	눈앞이 캄캄하다
three brothers	삼형제	to be hungry	배가 고프다
three days	사흘	to be in the air	소문이 나다
three kinds of	세 가지	to be jealous	질투하다
three times	세 번	to be just as it was	감쪽같다
three years	삼 년	to be kind	착하다
tiger	호랑이	to be late into	깊은 밤
to allow	허락하다	the night	
to amaze/admire at	감탄하다	to be lonely	외롭다
to answer	대답하다	to be mad	화가 나다
to apologize	사과하다	to be making	만들고 있다
to appear	나타나다	to be manic	정신없다
to appreciate	고마워하다	to be naïve	어리숙하다
to arrive	도착하다	to be not working	잘 되지 않다
to ask	물어보다	well	
to ask	묻다	to be offered	바쳐지다
to awake	깨다	(as a sacrifice)	
to be a fool	모자라다	to be old/older	나이가 많다
to be a lot	많다	to be over, past	넘다
to be awakened	깨다	to be pathetic	불쌍하다
from sleep		to be pitiful	가엾다
to be beautiful	예쁘다	to be plausible	그럴듯하다
to be born	태어나다	to be poor	가난하다
to be broken	부러지다	to be prepared (food)	차려져 있다
to be careful	조심하다	to be pretty	예쁘다
to be caught and	잡혀오다	to be punished	벌을 받다
brought		to be sad/disappointed	섭섭하다
to be changed	변하다	to be salty	짜지다
to be clean	깨끗하다	to be same	똑같다
to be cool	멋지다	to be sharp, pointy	뾰족하다
to be crazy	미치다	to be sick	아프다
to be curious	궁금하다	to be slow	느리다
to be dented	찌그러지다	to be smart	똑똑하다
to be different,	다른	to be sold	팔리다
another		to be strong	힘이 세다
to be dumbfounded	어이가 없다	to be sunny	화창하다
to be embarrassed	당황하다	to be surprised	놀라다
to be expensive	비싸다	to be three-forked	세 갈래
to be fast	빠르다	to be unhappy	불행하다
to be full of news	입이 근질근질하다	to be very interested	귀가 솔깃해지다
to be good at playing	(장구를) 잘 치다	to be warm	따뜻하다
to be greedy	욕심이 많다	to become	되다

to become … (negative)	~이 되고 말다
to become bigger	쑥쑥 자라다
to become clean	깨끗해지다
to become excited	신이 나다
to become heavy	무거워지다
to become shorter	짧아지다
to beg for food (and eat it)	얻어먹다
to believe	믿다
to bite	깨물다
to bite	물어뜯다
to bleed	피를 흘리다
to bow	절을 하다
to break	망가지다
to bring (a person from somewhere)	데려오다
to bring (a person to)	데려가다
to bring (from)	가져오다
to bring (to)	가져다주다
to build	짓다
to burn to death	불태워 죽이다
to bury/ be stained with	묻다
to buy	사다
to call	부르다
to care about	신경쓰다
to carry (someone) on your back	업다
to carry with	가지고 다니다
to catch	잡다
to catch and bring a person	잡아오다
to change	변하다
to chase	쫓아오다
to clap	손뼉을 치다
to climb	올라가다
to collapse	무너지다
to come	오다
to come back	돌아오다
to come in	들어오다
to come out	나오다
to come to hang out	놀러 오다
to correct one's bad habit	버릇을 고치다
to crawl	엉금엉금
to crawl into	기어들어오다
to cry	울다
to cut (down)	자르다/베다
to cut wood	나무를 하다
to dedicate	바치다
to die	죽다
to die (*honorific*)	돌아가시다
to dig	파다
to disappear	사라지다
to disappear without a trace	연기처럼 사라지다
to discover/to find	발견하다
to do as someone is told	그대로 하다
to do cartwheels	재주를 넘다
to do one's filial duty	효도하다
to do wrong	잘못하다
to draw back the bowstring	활시위를 당기다
to dream	꿈을 꾸다
to dress up well	잘 차려 입다
to drive away	쫓아 버리다
to drop	떨어뜨리다
to earn money	돈을 벌다
to eat	먹다
to eat oneself up	속이 새까맣게 타다
to enjoy	즐기다
to explain	설명하다
to fall	떨어지다/빠지다
to fall asleep	잠들다
to fall down	넘어지다/쓰러지다
to fart	방귀를 뀌다
to feel bad	기분이 나빠지다
to feel envious (*idiom*)	배가 아프다
to feel sorry	안타까워 하다
to feel sudden relief	앓던 이가 빠지는 것 같다
to find	찾다
to fly (away)	날아가다
to follow (come)	따라오다
to follow (go)	따라가다
to get angry	화를 내다
to get better	낫다
to get bigger and bigger	점점 커지다
to get sick	아프다
to give	주다
to give back, return	돌려주다

to give birth	낳다	to make	만들다
to give nothing	아무것도 주지	to marry	결혼하다
to give up	포기하다	to meet	만나다
to go	가다	to mess up/spoil	망치다
to go (past tense)	갔다	to miss (somebody)	그리워하다
to go back	돌아가다	to not believe	믿지 않다
to go late (past tense)	늦게 갔다	to not like	좋아하지 않다
to go off on a journey	여행을 떠나다	to not wash	씻지 않다
to go outside	밖에 나가다	to offer (a sacrifice)	바치다
to go to work	일하러 가다	to open	열다
to grant a wish	들어 주다	to order	명령하다
to grow longer	길어지다	to part	헤어지다
to grow up	자라다	to pass around, share	나누어 주다
to grudge something	아깝다	to pass by	지나가다
to harass	괴롭히다	to pay back money	돈을 갚다
to hate	싫어하다	to pile up	많아지다
to have	가지다	to play	놀다
to have a foul mouth	말버릇이 나쁘다	to poke	쿡쿡 찌르다
to have fallen	쓰러져 있다	to praise	칭찬하다
to help	도와주다/돕다	to pray	기도하다
to hide	숨다	to pretend ~	~척 하다
to hide (someone)	숨겨 주다	to pretend to be calm	아무렇지 않은 척 하다
to hit	치다/때리다		
to hurt	아프다	to pretend you don't know	모르는 척 하다
to invade	침략하다		
to jump up	뛰어오르다	to prey on	잡아먹다
to keep (doing something)	계속	to push	밀다
		to put	넣어 주다
to kick out	쫓아내다	to put it into somewhere	넣다
to kill	죽이다		
to knock	두드리다	to put something in	넣어 두다
to know nothing	아무것도 모르다	to receive	받다
to laugh	웃다	to regret	후회하다
to lay down	눕다	to repay	갚다
to learn	배우다	to repay one's kindness	은혜를 갚다
to lend money	돈을 빌리다		
to let someone go	보내주다	to return	돌아가다
to let someone stay	재워 주다	to reward	상을 주다
to lie face down	엎드리다	to ring	울리다
to lift something easily	번쩍 들다	to rise (the moon or sun)	뜨다
to like	좋아하다		
to like each other	서로 좋아하다	to root up	뽑아 버리다
to listen	듣다	to row	노를 젓다
to live	살다	to run (to someone)	뛰어오다
to live (lit., eat and live)	먹고 살다	to run away	달아나다/도망가다
to live happily	행복하게 살다	to rush	재촉하다
to look	쳐다보다	to say	말하다
to look the same	똑같이 생기다	to say hi	인사하다

to say let's do something	하자고 하다	to think something	~라고 생각하다
to say thank you	고맙다고 하다	to throw	던지다
to scold	야단치다	to throw someone out	내쫓다
to scoop rice	밥을 푸다	to tie	묶다
to scream	소리를 지르다	to tie up tightly	꽉 묶다
to see	보다	to travel	여행하다
to seek/find	구하다	to use it for what	어디에 쓰려고
to sell	팔다	to visit	방문하다/찾아오다
to separate	떨어뜨리다	to wail	대성통곡
to shoot (past tense)	쏘다	to wait	기다리다
to show a person to a room	방으로 안내하다	to walk	걷다
		to wander	돌아다니다
to show off	자랑을 하다	to want	원하다
to sigh	한숨을 쉬다	to want to have	가지고 싶다
to sing	노래를 부르다	to want to marry	결혼하고 싶다
to sing well	노래를 잘 하다	to wave (a fan)	(부채를) 부치다
to sink	가라앉다	to wear	입다
to skip a meal entirely	쫄쫄 굶다	to wear	쓰다
to sleep	자다	to weep, shed a few tears	훌쩍 훌쩍 울다
to sleep over	자고 가다		
to sleep late (past tense)	늦게 잤다	to win	이기다
		to whip	채찍질하다
to smell	냄새/(냄새)맡다	to wipe away	닦아 주다
to smile	웃다	to wish	원하다
to spare one's life	살려 주다	to work	일하다
to spill	엎지르다	to work/a work	일
to spin	돌리다	to worry	걱정하다
to split/share	나누다	to wring	비틀다
to stand on one's shoulders	목말을 타다	to write	적다
		to yell out	소리치다
to start on one's way	출발하다	toad	두꺼비
to steal	훔치다	together	함께/같이
to stomp on	밟다	top/above	위
to stop	멈추다	tournament	대회
to take (away)	가져가다	traditional party	잔치
to take someone everywhere	가져가다	treasure	보물
		tree	나무
to take care of someone	보살펴 주다	twenty times	스무 번
		twice	두 번
to talk about it everywhere	떠들고 다니다	two	두- / 둘
		two people	두 명
to talk through his hat	큰소리를 치다		
to tease	놀리다	**U**	
to tell	들려 주다	unaware of something (negative)	그것도 모르고
to think	생각하다		
to think about	~에 대해 생각하다	until now	이제까지

V

very	아주
village	마을 / 동네
village across a mountain	산 너머 마을

W

warehouse	창고
warm rice cake	따뜻한 떡
water	물
weather	날씨
well	우물
west	서쪽
when you were young	어렸을 때
where	어디
whip (noun)	채찍
why	왜
willow tree	버드나무
winter	겨울
wise	똑똑하다
wish	소원
without changing countenance	얼굴색 한번 바꾸지 않고
without knowing it	그것도 모르고
woman	여자
wood	나무
woodcutter	나무꾼
worry	걱정
wrapping cloth	보자기

Y

younger brother	남동생

Published by Tuttle Publishing, an imprint of Periplus Editions (HK) Ltd.

www.tuttlepublishing.com

Copyright © 2018 by Julie Damron

Audio recordings by Kim Kyuri
Illustrations by Megan Young and TJ Bae

LCCN 2020277447

ISBN 978-0-8048-5003-2

Distributed by

North America, Latin America & Europe
Tuttle Publishing
364 Innovation Drive
North Clarendon, VT 05759-9436 U.S.A.
Tel: 1 (802) 773-8930; Fax: 1 (802) 773-6993
info@tuttlepublishing.com; www.tuttlepublishing.com

Japan
Tuttle Publishing
Yaekari Building 3rd Floor
5-4-12 Osaki
Shinagawa-ku
Tokyo 141 0032
Tel: (81) 3 5437-0171; Fax: (81) 3 5437-0755
sales@tuttle.co.jp; www.tuttle.co.jp

Asia Pacific
Berkeley Books Pte. Ltd.
3 Kallang Sector #04-01
Singapore 349278
Tel: (65) 6741-2178; Fax: (65) 6741-2179
inquiries@periplus.com.sg; www.tuttlepublishing.com

First edition
27 26 25 24   12 11 10   2403TP   Printed in Singapore

TUTTLE PUBLISHING® is a registered trademark of Tuttle Publishing, a division of Periplus Editions (HK) Ltd.

"Books to Span the East and West"

Tuttle Publishing was founded in 1832 in the small New England town of Rutland, Vermont [USA]. Our core values remain as strong today as they were then—to publish best-in-class books which bring people together one page at a time. In 1948, we established a publishing outpost in Japan—and Tuttle is now a leader in publishing English-language books about the arts, languages and cultures of Asia. The world has become a much smaller place today and Asia's economic and cultural influence has grown. Yet the need for meaningful dialogue and information about this diverse region has never been greater. Over the past seven decades, Tuttle has published thousands of books on subjects ranging from martial arts and paper crafts to language learning and literature—and our talented authors, illustrators, designers and photographers have won many prestigious awards. We welcome you to explore the wealth of information available on Asia at **www.tuttlepublishing.com**.